LIQUID HISTORY

THE 'THOMAS KING' ENTERING LONDON DOCK, 1827

With the first cargo of sugar from the West Indies after the expiration of the exclusive privilege of the West India Dock Company
Oil painting by *William John Huggins (1781-1845)* *Collection of the Port of London Authority*

LIQUID HISTORY

To commemorate Fifty Years of the

Port of London Authority

1909–1959

BY ARTHUR BRYANT

PRIVATELY PRINTED

LONDON 1960

TEXT SET IN 12 PT MONOTYPE IMPRINT

PRINTED IN ENGLAND AT

THE CURWEN PRESS · PLAISTOW · LONDON · E.13

CONTENTS

LIST OF ILLUSTRATIONS

LIQUID HISTORY

The words 'Liquid History' used for the title of this book originate with the Rt. Hon. John Burns P.C.

A Canadian from the banks of the great St. Lawrence and an American from the banks of the great Missouri asked, rather derisively, John Burns's comparative view of the St. Lawrence, the Missouri, and the River Thames. John Burns replied:

The St. Lawrence is mere water. The Missouri muddy water. The Thames is liquid history.

Other origins for the expression were advanced but on 4 October 1929 the precise facts as stated above were written on a sheet of paper by John Burns and initialled 'Best wishes J.B.'.

The document is preserved in the Library of the Port of London Authority.

INTRODUCTION

THIS study has been written to tell, in outline, the story of the Port of London Authority during the first half-century of its existence. That half-century has witnessed two world wars—in the second of which the Port became for a time the principal target in Hitler's bid for world dominion—and a most far-reaching social and industrial revolution. Yet, though the purpose of this brief record has been to summarize the achievement of the Authority in its administration and development of the Port and to trace the Port's growth in modern times, that growth—as the P.L.A. has always recognized—is the outcome of two thousand years of history. I have tried, therefore, in my opening pages to show how the Port began and grew and how the legislative changes which resulted in 1909 in the foundation of the Port of London Authority were the natural outcome of what had gone before. That that outcome has proved so fortunate, despite the immense difficulties the Authority has had to face, is a proof of the national genius for creating continuing institutions capable both of inspiring loyalty and devotion in those who serve them and of adapting themselves to the needs of a constantly changing world.

ARTHUR BRYANT

'It is notorious that the river of Thames is so necessary, commodious and practicable to the City of London that without the said river our City could not long subsist, flourish and continue.'

Royal Charter of King James I.

'All alone I went a-walking by the London Docks one day,
For to see the ships discharging in the basins where they lay;
And the cargoes that I saw there they were every sort and kind,
Every blessed brand of merchandise a man could bring to mind;
There were things in crates and boxes, there was stuff in bags
 and bales,
There were tea-chests wrapped in matting, there were
                    Eastern-looking frails,
There were baulks of teak and greenheart, there were stacks
 of spruce and pine,
There was cork and frozen carcasses and casks of Spanish wine,
There was rice and spice and cocoa-nuts, and rum enough was
 there
For to warm all London's innards up and leave a drop to spare.'

C. Fox-Smith.

The Thames Highway

NEARLY a hundred years ago the French historian, Taine, visiting England in 1861, described a voyage which he made up the Thames to London.

'Gravesend on the left heaps its brown houses around a blueish steeple. Vessels, warehouses, increase in number. One feels that one is approaching a great city. The small landing-stages project fifty paces into the river over the shining mud which the fallen tide leaves dry. Every quarter of an hour, the imprint and the presence of man, the power by which he has transformed nature, become more visible; docks, magazines, ship-building and caulking yards, stocks, habitable houses, prepared materials, accumulated merchandise; to the right is seen the skeleton of an iron church which is being prepared here for erection in India. Astonishment ends by turning into bewilderment. From Greenwich, the river is nothing but a street a mile broad and upwards, where ships ascend and descend between two rows of buildings, interminable rows of a dull red, in brick or tiles, bordered with great piles stuck in the mud for mooring vessels, which come here to unload or to load. Ever new magazines for copper, stone, coal, cordage, and the rest; bales are always being piled up, sacks being hoisted, barrels being rolled, cranes are creaking, capstans sounding. The sea reaches London by the river; it is an inland port; New York, Melbourne, Canton, Calcutta, are in direct connection with this place. But that which carries the impression to its height, is the sight of the canals through which the docks communicate with the sea; they form cross-streets, and they are streets for ships; one suddenly perceives a line of them which is endless; from Greenwich Park where I ascended last year, the horizon is bounded with masts and ropes. The incalculable indistinct rigging stretches a spider's web in a circle at the side of the sky. This is certainly one of the great spectacles of our planet; to see a similar conglomeration of erections, of men, of vessels, and of business, it would be necessary to go to China.

On the river to the west, rises an inextricable forest of yards, of masts, of rigging; these are the vessels which arrive, depart or anchor, in the first place in groups, then in long rows, then in a continuous heap, crowded together, massed against the chimneys of houses and the pulleys of warehouses, with all the tackle of incessant, regular, gigantic labour. A foggy smoke penetrated with light envelopes them; the sun there sifts its golden rain, and the brackish, tawny, half-green, half-violet water, balances in its undulations striking and strange reflections. It might be said this was the heavy and smoky air of a large hothouse. Nothing is natural here, everything is transformed, artificially wrought from the toil of man, up to the light and the air. But the hugeness of the conglomeration and of the human creation hinders us from thinking about this deformity and this artifice; for want of pure and healthy beauty, the swarming and grandiose life remains; the shimmering of embrowned waves, the scattering of the light imprisoned in vapour, the soft whitish or pink tints which cover these vastnesses, diffuse a sort of grace over the prodigious city, having the effect of a smile upon the face of a shaggy and blackened Cyclop.'[1]

Ninety-eight years after Taine wrote this account of the river and docks, the Port of London Authority celebrated, in 1959, its fiftieth anniversary. Under its rule the flow of maritime trade—far greater even than when the French historian witnessed it—is still maintained without cessation, but the dingy chaos he described and that his countryman, Gustave Doré, drew in his infernal pictures of Victorian dockland, has been banished and replaced by order, spaciousness and cleanliness. Here with a water area of nearly seven hundred acres and thirty-six miles of quay, are five vast dock groups, with cargo-handling mechanism of the most modern kind operated by a skilled and regularly employed labour force whose average weekly wage today is in the neighbourhood of £17 and which in a few cases can rise to as much as

[1] Hippolyte Taine, *Notes on England*.

£30 a week. Additional labour is drawn from the pool
maintained by the National Dock Labour Board as occasion
demands. The only congestion normally visible on the
Authority's premises is that of the parked cars of dockers
and dock employees, a large proportion of whom arrive
every morning by motor or motor-cycle. Yet the ceaseless
import, export and storage of merchandise never pauses, an
average of more than a million tons of which is handled in
the Port every week.

The P.L.A., which has performed this miracle, does its
work, like the Port itself, out of sight of the vast majority of
Londoners, most of whom have neither heard of it and, if
they have, have only the vaguest notion of what it is and
does. Yet on its work the prosperity of almost every Londoner indirectly depends. Had Hitler in 1940 been able to
put the Port and its administration permanently out of action
it could have proved even more fatal to this country than the
destruction of the Ruhr proved to Germany. For more than
any other nation, Britain lives by the sea and seaborne trade,
and it is into the Port of London that a third of that trade
flows. London is the Venice of the modern world. Though
no contrast could be greater than between the appearance of
the two cities, what Venice was to the commerce of the
medieval Mediterranean, grey, smoky London and her
river are to the ocean trade of our age.

What a romance is here, and how much of the history of
our country is comprised in it! For sixty-nine miles of
tideway, from the seaward limit six miles east of Southend
to Teddington, the great Port in all its ramifications, from
huge modern docks to tiny ancient jetties, from 35,000-ton
liners to slow, grubby lighters and minute, darting launches,
continues to serve the daily life and needs of every one of us.
Only the seagulls descending on the ornamental waters of
the central London parks or the sound at night of sirens and

fog-horns remind the Londoner of its existence and of the ceaseless traffic done on the waters and quaysides of 'Old Father Thames'. For that much sung ballad enshrines an unchanging truth. Out of the river and its trade has sprung London's history.

CHAPTER ONE

The Port's Beginnings

THE Port's story began two thousand years ago when a trading settlement sprang up at the first point above the sea where it was possible, at low water, to bridge the tidal Thames. Here, where a gravel eminence on the north bank approached a gravel ledge projecting from the Southwark marshes, was a deep pool where ships could lie, and it was from the Celtic words Llyn-Din—'the hill by the pool'—that some suppose that London derived its name. It was at this point, about the time that Christ was living in Palestine, traders from the Continent seem to have established some kind of seaborne exchange with the Celtic tribesmen of southern Britain.

It was probably in protection of this trade that in A.D. 43 the Roman legions, under the Emperor Claudius, invaded the island and incorporated southern Britain in the Roman Empire. Eighteen years later, when a rising of the Celtic tribesmen occurred, the historian Tacitus wrote of London as 'a colony much frequented by merchants and trading vessels'. During the next three and a half centuries—a period almost twice as long as the British occupation of India—*Londinium* was the largest city in the island, owing its wealth and importance, not like the other Roman cities of Britain to the imperial military and administrative hierarchy, but to seaborne commerce. As the furthest point in the interior to which ships from the Continent could penetrate, it became the focus of the island's earliest road system. And when in the fifth century Roman civilization collapsed and

B

Britain was submerged under a tide of invasions by Germanic sea-pirates, London survived behind its fortifications—'a great inland haven guarded by walls'—and preserved, in a barbaric age, some vestige of its former Roman and commercial character. The Venerable Bede, the earliest Anglo-Saxon chronicler, described it as being in A.D. 605—eight years after St. Augustine and his missionaries landed in Kent—'a market for many nations repairing to them by land and sea', and the capital of the East Saxon kingdom of Essex. At this period it seems to have imported timber, resin and wine in exchange for corn and wool, the island's two principal products.

By the time that the great West Saxon king, Alfred—the Churchill of the Dark Ages—established three centuries later, for the first time since the Romans, a single unified State in southern Britain, it was commercial London, rather than his native capital, Winchester, that he made the focus of the England he had saved from the Vikings. For London was England's gateway to the sea, and, with his wonderful vision, Alfred—an inspired ruler if ever there was one—knew that England's future must be by sea. The little East Saxon port which he incorporated with such far-reaching results into his realm was based on the creeks of the Fleet and Walbrook streams which flowed southward into the Thames, the one without, the other within London's ancient Roman walls. The hithes, wharves and landing-places—Queenhithe, Dowgate, Billingsgate—along the river-front were minute by modern standards, but they lay at the foot of streets and alleys that ran into the heart of the city and linked its life with that of the river and sea. During the greater part of its existence and long after it had expanded westwards and eastwards beyond its Roman walls, London remained primarily a riverside port, a long narrow city hugging the Thames from which it drew its nurture.

In those remote Saxon times the Port's trade must have been very precarious, carried on through pirate-haunted seas with the river-ports of the dissolving Frankish Empire on the far side of the Channel. We know that merchants, mostly foreign, imported wine and fish from Rouen and pepper and spices from Antwerp—brought at incredible risk by camel, dhow and galley from the Far East—and that 'far-coming men', as they were called, in strange, brightly-coloured clothes, had special places where they traded their wares in London. Such were the Vintry where the vintners of Rouen congregated, Eastcheap with its Ghent and Ponthieu gold-smiths, Dowgate with clothiers from Flanders and Cologne. We know, too, that as they came up the river in their tiny ships freighted with Rhenish wines, the seamen of Lorraine sang a *kiriele* or signature-carol to show the watchers of the Port that they were friends. There were already English merchants, too, who travelled abroad in search of fortune or themselves owned ships. 'I go overseas,' one of them wrote, 'and buy purple and silk, precious gems and gold, many-coloured garments and dyes, wine and oil, ivory and brass, copper and tin, sulphur and glass.' Those who today bring the treasures of the globe to the Thames and store them in the warehouses of the Port of London have a long and heroic ancestry behind them.

Within a century of Alfred's death the Vikings, from whom he saved England, were again harrying the kingdom he had created. Yet however terrible their depredations, the character of these fierce Scandinavian pirates was changing. They loved war and plunder, but they loved trade even more. One of Alfred's greatest achievements had been to convert those who had already settled in England to Christianity, and in 1016 a christianized Viking conqueror from Denmark, Canute, was elected by the English Witan— among whose members were the merchant aldermen or 'naval men of London', as they were called—as King of all England. As he was also ruler of most of Scandinavia, one result of his accession was a large increase in trade between London and the Baltic. It is a trade that has continued to this day, as any visitor to the great timber wharves and sheds of the Surrey Commercial Docks can see for himself.

CHAPTER TWO

Medieval Thames-side

THOUGH under Canute, it looked as though all the
seafaring peoples of the North Sea littoral were about
to be linked in a loose maritime union with London
as their capital, England's destiny and London's did not lie
in a Scandinavian empire circling the North Sea. It lay for
the next four centuries in an Anglo-French one astride the
Channel. Canute's empire dissolved almost immediately
after his death and the old West Saxon dynasty resumed its
rule of southern Britain. But in 1066 it fell, and England
with it, to an invasion by the Duke of Normandy, whose
mounted knights, half-French, half-Viking, destroyed King
Harold and the English army at Hastings. And it was to 'the
burghers within London, French and English friendly'—
that is, to its sea-traders—that William the Conqueror held
out the hand of friendship as the surest way to cement his
victory. The Norman merchants, who both preceded and
accompanied him and whose descendants intermarried with
the English, henceforward became an increasingly important
element in the life of London. In the century after the
Conquest one of them, who served as London's portreeve
or mayor, became the father of the greatest English hero of
the Middle Ages, Thomas à Becket—the Archbishop of
Canterbury who suffered martyrdom in his own cathedral.

Becket's chaplain and biographer, William Fitz-Stephen,
himself a Londoner, has left us our best picture of the City
and the Port at this time. 'To this City,' he wrote, 'merchants

bring in wares by ships from every nation under Heaven.
The Arabian sends his gold, the Sabean his frankincense
and spices, the Scythian arms and oil of palms from the
plentiful wood; Babylon her fat soil and Nilus his precious
stones; the Seres send purple garments; they of Norway
and Russia trouts, furs and sables; and the French their
wines.' This was perhaps an exaggeration, but the trade of
the Thames was already formidable. To control it and ensure
the collection of their royal tolls and customs as well as to
dominate the City, the Conqueror and his successors built
and maintained a stone tower on the little hill immediately
to the east of the Pool, commanding the river approaches to
the City's quays and wharves. It is on this eminence beside
the Tower that the Port of London Authority's offices today
stand.

Above the Tower and the Pool and where the old ford to
Southwark lay, the London traders about the time of
Becket's martyrdom began to build a stone bridge in place
of an earlier wooden one that had been burnt down. With
twenty narrow arches supported by piers on 'sterlings' sunk
in the river bed, it was finished in King John's reign—six
years before Magna Carta—and effected a revolution,
unforeseen by its builders, in the life of the Port. For
though it was equipped with a drawbridge to allow for the
passage of masted ships and to prevent an invading force
from entering the City, the rapids created by its piers made
it both difficult and dangerous for vessels to reach the
ancient City quays from the sea. As a result the axis of the
Port of London moved downstream into the Pool immediately below bridge. Crowned with houses, shops and towers
and normally passed only by wherries and barges manned by
highly skilled and specially licensed watermen, the bridge—
which was to survive for seven centuries, almost into the
lifetime of the parents of men and women still living—

increasingly separated the life and work of the City above it from the resort of sea-going ships below, whose masts crowded London's eastern skyline and whose freights were the source of its wealth.

So began the second phase in the Port's history—one that was to last for six centuries, from the time of Edward I to the closing years of George III's reign and the long struggle against Napoleon. Throughout all this long stretch of time London's seaborne merchandise was mainly loaded to and from ships moored in the deep waters of the Pool or, when the latter became too congested, in the river below it, and was thence carried by barge or wherry to the hithes, quays and warehouses of the City above bridge. Of the older hithes only Billingsgate, lying as it did below the bridge and overlooking the Pool, could conveniently accommodate sea-going vessels at its wharves, with the result that Queen-hithe—hitherto the principal 'strand' for landing and loading goods in the heart of the City—declined in importance. It was at Billingsgate and in its adjoining inlets or 'docks' that the King's customs officers did their work, assessing and levying tolls on merchandise brought into or exported from England, while the City's officers collected tolls and dues on domestic merchandise for the maintenance of the Port and bridge. Among the royal customs officers was at one time the first of the great English poets, Geoffrey Chaucer, who, the son of a London vintner and born, it is believed, in a house in Thames Street at the foot of Dowgate Hill, was appointed in 1374 Comptroller of the Customs of Wool, Skins and Tanned Hides—then the country's principal export—in the City of London. It was probably from the types with whom he came into contact in his London life and work that this highly original genius drew the characters of his Canterbury pilgrims. One of them, it will be recalled, was the Shipman:

> Hardy he was and wise to undertake,
> With many a tempest hath his beard been shake,
> He knew well all the havens, as they were,
> From Scotland to the Cape of Finisterre,
> And every creek in Brittany and Spain;
> His bark y-clepèd was the *Magdalen*.

One can picture the poet as he supervised his subordinates on the wharves, while they made their tallies on the goods carried ashore—'the wine of Spain that creepeth subtilly' and 'white wine of Oseye and red wine of Gascoigne, of the Rhine and of the Rochelle'.

The site of the P.L.A. building on Tower Hill could not thus be more historically appropriate, looking down over a riverside haunted by the ghosts, not only of Geoffrey Chaucer, but of every man who contributed to London's seaborne commerce for the six centuries when Billingsgate and the Pool were the heart of her port. It was a period that saw a vast expansion of maritime trade: beginning in the thirteenth and fourteenth centuries with the export of raw wool from English sheep-walks to the cloth towns of Flanders and Northern Italy and growing during the latter Middle Ages and Tudor epoch into an immensely profitable export of finished cloth to Europe. At first the trade of the Port was still comparatively small—its exports corn, raw wool, fat cattle, hides and herrings; its imports fine cloth from Flanders, wine from Gascony, Spain and the Rhineland, furs from Scandinavia, Damascus and Toledo blades from the Arab Empire and Spain; Baltic timber and German silver and armour; spices, gold and jewels from Venice and the Orient. Much of it passed through the hands of foreign merchants who lived and traded under royal protection, like the Lombard goldsmiths of Lombard Street and the German traders of the Hanseatic League or Easterlings as they were called, whose Steelyard in Thames Street—on the

plate ii

THE POOL OF LONDON, 1647

Fragment of 'The Long Bird's-Eye View of London', 1647 *Engraved by Wenceslaus Hollar*

Reproduced by courtesy of the Trustees of the British Museum

plate iii

BRUNSWICK DOCK ON THE THAMES AT BLACKWALL, 1803

Opened 1790 and 'chiefly intended for the accommodation and protection of the ships of the Honble. the East India Company'

Oil painting by William Daniell, R.A. (1769–1837)

Reproduced by courtesy of the Trustees of the National Maritime Museum

plate iv AN ELEVATED VIEW OF THE NEW DOCKS AND WAREHOUSES NOW CONSTRUCTING ON THE ISLE OF DOGS NEAR LIMEHOUSE FOR THE RECEPTION AND ACCOMMODATION OF SHIPPING IN THE WEST INDIA TRADE, 1802

Aquatint in colours, drawn and engraved by William Daniell, R.A.

Collection of the Port of London Authority

site of the present Cannon Street Station—was protected by walls from the turbulent London apprentices whose jealousy against the foreigner could be easily and terribly aroused.

During this time the conservancy of the Thames and the administration of the Port was vested in the City of London which from the days of the first Plantagenet kings had increasingly assumed control, through its elected officers and councillors, of its own affairs, including the levying of mercantile tolls and dues. 'From time out of mind', ran one of its Charters, 'the Mayor, commonalty and citizens of the City of London have exercised the office of bailiff and conservators of the Thames from Staines Bridge to Yantlet and in the Medway and in the Port of the City of London, upon each bank and every shore and upon every wharf.' Its officials had the right to measure and levy charges on all coal, grain, salt, fruit, vegetables and other goods and merchandise sold by measure, that were brought into the Port. By a Charter of Edward IV, who established a close bond between the Court and City, the Corporation was given a monopoly of packing woollen cloths, skins and other goods, the garbling—or grading—of all spices, the carriage of wine between the port and the vintners' cellars, and the porterage of all merchandise between the Thames and the warehouses of the foreign merchants in the City. Many of the functions which are today exercised by the officers and craftsmen of the Port of London Authority were thus being exercised in a different form by the officers of the City five hundred years ago.

CHAPTER THREE

The Legal Quays

I T was in the sixteenth century that the trade and shipping of London River first assumed the world-wide importance that it has enjoyed ever since. With the discovery of America and of the ocean trade routes to India and the Far East during the reign of the first Tudor king, the focus of Europe's commerce and wealth began to shift from the Mediterranean ports of Venice and Genoa, with their links with the Arab caravan trade of the Middle East, and became centred on the western or Atlantic littoral of Europe, notably on Cadiz, Lisbon, Antwerp and, after the accession of Queen Elizabeth, on London and the Devon, Cornish and Bristol Channel ports. Henceforward, instead of being on the furthest circumference of the known world, England was at its centre. During the forty-five years of Elizabeth's prudent yet highly adventurous reign, and even in those of her father and grandfather, English seamen and merchants increasingly staked a claim to share in the wealth of the new trade with America and the Indies that the Pope had attempted to keep as a monopoly of the Catholic and maritime Empires of Spain and Portugal. Throughout the last four decades of the sixteenth century a series of expeditions, financed by London and West of England merchants and some of them, though secretly, by the Queen herself, sailed from London River and the Western ports to discover a passage to the Orient round the northern shores of Europe and America and to participate, by force if necessary, in the

enormously profitable trade of the subjects of the Kings of
Spain and Portugal with Central and South America, the
West and East Indies, Africa, Ceylon and India. It was out
of such voyages that sprang, not only the defeat of the
Spanish Armada that was Spain's disastrous response to
this English challenge, but the foundation of the English
Muscovy, Africa, Turkey and Hudson's Bay Companies and,
most momentous of all, of the East India and Virginia
Companies.

It was to ensure for the Crown its due share of the
expanding ocean wealth and to prevent leakage in Customs
duties, that Elizabeth's Government, at the outset of her
reign, set up a Royal Commission to select and appoint
licensed wharves where all dutiable goods entering the
country should be exclusively landed. The twenty 'Legal
Quays', as they were designated, appropriated in London for
this purpose, henceforward enjoyed an official monopoly
which, with modifications, lasted for two and a half centuries.
All were sited along the north bank of the river between
London Bridge and the Tower, seven to the west of Billingsgate, and thirteen to the east of it, and their names—Brewers
quay, Chesters quay, Galley quay, Great and Little Bear
quays, Wool quay, Sabbs quay—became part of London's
history and of the language of seafaring men all the world over.
Here, in their little muddy creeks and in the warehouses
that tumbled down to the river on either side of them,
under surveillance of the Customs officers who daily attended them, there flowed into London and England the ocean
trade born of the discovery of the New World and of the
sea-passage to the Far East.

It was at this time, too, that London first began to assume
importance as a banking centre. Just as two centuries before,
the protection offered by an English king to Flemish weavers
had created the cloth trade, so during Elizabeth's reign a

new impetus was given to England's, and London's, commerce by the persecution by imperial Spain of the Protestant burghers of Holland and Northern Flanders who, in their hour of agony, turned to their co-religionists in England for protection and help. The sack of Antwerp in 1585 by the Duke of Alba's Spanish pikemen drove the gold—and, more important, the credit—of the Netherlands bankers into England and made London the financial centre of the world. Part of this achievement was due to the life work of a great London merchant, Sir Thomas Gresham, who for many years before the fall of Antwerp had been the Crown's financial agent there and whose sign of the Grasshopper outside his London house in Lombard Street, like the Royal Exchange he built for his native city, was to become part of London's permanent heritage. But it was her port and its trade that, first and foremost, made her a financial and banking city. The foundations of Threadneedle Street, it is no exaggeration to say, rest on the tides that throughout the ages have carried ships between London and the sea.

During the reign of Elizabeth—perhaps the most germinating in our history—three great events occurred in London River, all of them within what today is the jurisdiction of the Port of London Authority. The first was the knighting in 1580 of Sir Francis Drake on the deck of the *Golden Hind* as the little ship lay off Deptford after the termination of her wonderful voyage round the world. The second was the Queen's visit to Tilbury—now the passenger-terminus of the Port—while the Armada was coming up the Channel. The speech she made to her troops there epitomized for all time the spirit of England in peril. 'I know I have the body of a weak and feeble woman but I have the heart and stomach of a king and think foul scorn that any prince of Spain or Parma should dare to invade my realm. I will not be by violence constrained!'—words that have echoed again and again in our history and which have been made good by generations of British seamen. The third event, still more momentous, was the despatch from Woolwich on 13 February 1601 of the first trading fleet of the East India Company, chartered on the last day of 1600 after a meeting of London traders under the chairmanship of the Lord Mayor, to challenge the Dutch and Portuguese monopoly of trade to the Far East. From this Thames-side venture sprang in the fullness of time the British Empire in India.

Nor is it without significance that during these years the plays of William Shakespeare were being performed for the first time in the Globe Theatre, a stone's throw from London Bridge and close to the crowded ships lying in the Pool. Among those who watched the plays of Shakespeare, Marlowe and their contemporaries, must have been many of the seamen who sailed from London to find new worlds beyond the seas. The storm in *The Tempest* was founded on a real storm and shipwreck that befell a London ship in 'the still-vexed Bermoothes' on her way to Virginia in 1609. And when Shakespeare drew the rich Venetian merchant, Antonio, with 'mind tossing on the ocean',

> Plucking the grass to know where sits the wind,
> Peering in maps for ports, and piers, and roads;

it was not of Venice's lagoons and the Rialto he was thinking but of Gresham's new Royal Exchange and the little 'Legal Quays' along the Thames to which the argosies of London's merchant adventurers returned from a world of storms and pirates and of trading for silks and spices in the furthest corners of the earth. Such were worthy citizens of credit and renown, who during the reigns of Elizabeth's two successors played a leading part in the foundation of what today is the United States and with whose successors, a generation later, Pepys dined in London taverns, and whose minds, for all their peaceful City days spent within sound of Bow bells, were with their fortunes, voyaging in ships with portholes 'opening on the foam of perilous seas in faery lands forlorn'.

plate v

WEST INDIA DOCKS FROM THE SOUTH-EAST, 1830

Coloured lithograph by William Parrott
Collection of the Port of London Authority

plate vi

THE OPENING OF ST. KATHARINE DOCK, 25 OCTOBER 1828

Oil painting by William John Huggins (1781–1845)

Collection of the Port of London Authority

CHAPTER FOUR

Chaos on the River

SIXTY years after Elizabeth's death, Charles II declared that 'the thing that is nearest the heart of this nation is trade and all that belongs to it'. 'Martha, Martha', wrote his great Minister, Lord Halifax, 'thou art busy about many things; to the question what shall we do to be saved in this world, there is no other answer but this, "Look to your moat!" The first article of an Englishman's creed is that he believes in the sea.' During the century that followed the defeat of the Armada, when King and Parliament, Episcopalian and Puritan, were engaged in bitter political and religious controversies, English merchants and seamen were steadily expanding the country's commerce and creating colonies and trading settlements on the shores of North America and in the West and East Indies. During this period the 'Legal Quays', with their highly profitable monopoly, were kept increasingly busy, and by the time that, with the Revolution of 1688 and the accession of William III, Parliament had established its right to legislative supremacy, the concourse of ships in London River had become far greater than could be accommodated by those twenty small quays between the Bridge and Tower. The Pool itself was by now too small for all the ships that traded in the Thames; the Port of London, out of sheer necessity, was beginning to move down the river, beyond the confines of London itself, and into the Lower Pool and Limehouse Reach. In 1612, only nine years after Elizabeth's death and six after three London ships sailed to found the first

c

permanent English colony in North America, the East India
Company established its shipping headquarters at Blackwall.
Half a century later, in the year after the Restoration,
Pepys, the diarist, went by water to visit a wet dock there—
the first recorded on the Thames. It was only an acre and
a half in extent and used, not for the landing of goods, which
still had to be taken ashore at the 'Legal Quays', but for the
launching and fitting out of East Indiamen. But in the last
decade of the century—a generation after the temporary
destruction in the Great Fire of London of every wharf and
warehouse on the north bank—an enclosed dock, 1,070 feet
long and 500 feet wide and covering ten acres of water, was
built under a private Act of Parliament in the Surrey fields
at Rotherhithe, half a mile below the Lower Pool. It was
named the Howland Great Wet Dock after the lady—a
daughter of Sir Josiah Child, the famous East India merchant—who owned the land on which it was built and from
whom its possession passed for a time by marriage to the
Dukes of Bedford. Its builders claimed that, when full, it
held over a quarter of a million tons of water, 'being much
larger than the famous bason of Dunkirk or any pent water
in the world', and that upward of 120 sail of the largest
merchant ships could lie in it 'without the trouble of
shifting, mooring or unmooring any in the dock for taking
in or out any other'. It boasted, too, a great crane 'for taking
out and setting in masts in ships in the wet dock, which
answers the end of a hulk with proper pits and crab for
careening three or four ships at once'. It may have been of
this dock, opened in the early part of Queen Anne's reign,
that Jonathan Swift was thinking when he described
Gulliver's exploit of towing off the assembled fleet and
transports of Blefuscu. During the great gale of November
1703—one of the worst ever recorded in England, when
nearly 700 ships anchored in the Thames were driven

ashore or damaged—only one vessel in the Howland Dock received any injury and that of a trifling kind. A quarter of a century later the Howland Wet Dock was adapted for the whaling trade, equipped with boilers and tanks for extracting oil from blubber, and renamed the Greenland Dock. A somewhat similar venture was the building in 1789 of the Perry or Brunswick Dock at Blackwall for fitting out East Indiamen, and which contained a building one hundred and twenty feet high for masting and dismantling ships.

Yet throughout the eighteenth century, as in the centuries before, the vast bulk of the shipping that carried the commerce of London continued to be accommodated in the open river. The result was ever-growing stagnation. In less than a hundred years London's seaborne trade quadrupled, but communication between ships and shore steadily worsened. By the time of the French Revolutionary Wars in the seventeen-nineties something like 14,000 voyages were being made from the Thames annually, that is at the rate of nearly forty a day. At times there were as many as seven or eight hundred ships moored in the Upper Pool at moorings designed at the most for five hundred, while vessels waited for a week or more to enter. With only a narrow channel, which had become so clogged with the discharge of ballast and sewage that incoming sugar ships were forced to unload part of their cargoes at Deptford, there was scarcely room in the crowded tideway for ships to move, while the delays in landing goods grew ever greater. Though London was by now the greatest port in the world and accounted for two-thirds of the country's seaborne trade, the total quay-frontage of the twenty 'Legal Quays' and of the twenty-one 'Sufferance Wharves', mostly on the Surrey shore, which had been licensed to supplement them, was less than 1,500 feet—or only a third of that of Bristol. As there was no room at the quays, ships had to be moored abreast in mid-stream, often four or five deep, while more than three thousand lighters and wherries continuously ferried their cargoes to and from the congested wharves, tacking athwart the river and making confusion worse confounded.

Even more serious than the delays caused by this congestion was the appalling loss of goods through theft. By the second half of the eighteenth century the river had become a thieves' paradise. Gangs of armed pirates cut loaded lighters adrift at night and stripped them when they came ashore; 'scuffle-hunters', as they were called, prowled the quays carrying off what they could filch from the piles of unguarded merchandise lying there, and 'mud-larks', who sometimes earned as much as £5 a night, collected goods from the water's edge thrown overboard by labourers or seamen in league with them. Thousands employed on the river were involved in this wholesale dishonesty, even ships' mates and revenue officers; it was reckoned that at least a quarter of the 'lumpers', as the labourers were called who loaded and unloaded ships, were either amateur pilferers or regular criminals. During the last decade of the century at least half a million pounds' worth of goods—a sum worth at least nine or ten times that amount in present-day money—was stolen annually. 'A bold, audacious system of plunder', Patrick Colquhoun, the Metropolitan Police magistrate and part-founder of the first Thames Marine Police Force, described it in his treatise on the Commerce and Police of the River.

CHAPTER FIVE

The Making of the Docks

THE only real remedy for the thieving and the congestion that was its cause was to end the monopoly of the ridiculously antiquated and inadequate 'Legal Quays' and 'Sufferance Wharves' and substitute, in place of the Pool and open river, enclosed docks where ships could lie in safety and load direct to the shore. Strangled by vested interests, riddled with crime and dishonesty and choked by the very success of the country's expanding commerce, the Port could only renew its life by being reborn. It was this realization that brought about in the last years of the eighteenth century and the first of the nineteenth the renaissance of the Port of London.

One of the forerunners of that renaissance was a London insurance director and Fellow of the Royal Society, named William Vaughan, who in 1793—the year of the outbreak of the wars with Revolutionary France—published a treatise *On Wet Docks, Quays and Warehouses for the Port of London, with hints respecting Trade*. In it he urged the construction of enclosed tide-free docks along the lower river between the Tower and Blackwall, suggesting as possible sites St. Katherine's in Wapping, the Isle of Dogs and, on the south bank, Rotherhithe. 'London', he wrote, 'is capable, from situation, to take the lead in docks'—a lead which at that moment was being taken by its rival in the West Indian trade, Liverpool. A few months later, in the spring of 1794, Vaughan convened a meeting of London merchants and chairmen of public bodies to consider the state of the

'Legal Quays'. A committee appointed by the meeting recommended that wet docks at Wapping would 'best tend to remove the difficulties and inconveniences which affected the commerce of the Port' and that a cut from Blackwall across the Poplar marshes or Isle of Dogs would prove of great service. It urged, too, that an immediate appeal for support should be made to the Corporation of the City and to the Government.

The upshot was a general subscription by London merchants and shipowners, a petition to Parliament and the appointment in 1796 of a Parliamentary Committee, of which the First Lord of the Treasury and Prime Minister, William Pitt, was a member, 'to enquire into the best Mode of providing sufficient Accommodation for the increased Trade and Shipping of the Port of London'. The Committee's report was made at the darkest moment of the war with France, in the year before Nelson, serving under Sir John Jervis at Cape St. Vincent, won the first of the dazzling sea victories that were to culminate eight years later in Trafalgar. Despite the powerful vested interest of the City Corporation, which had been the sole Port authority since the early Middle Ages and which at first strongly opposed any change in its time-honoured arrangements or lack of them, the arguments of the West India merchants—the chief sufferers from the system of pillage in the river— prevailed. The Committee, which sat for twenty-five days, heard evidence from every interest in the Port, including Trinity House, the Customs, the Admiralty, the East India Company, the proprietors of the 'Legal Quays', the Fire Offices, and representatives of the shipowners, merchants, wharfingers, City porters, carmen and lightermen. The conclusions it presented to the House were that the existing resources of the Port were inadequate for the purpose of its extended commerce and that they could only be rendered

depression and social unrest that followed the Napoleonic Wars, by the building of the St. Katharine Docks—opened by yet another private Dock Company in 1828—whose warehouses were specially designed to house and safeguard such valuable cargoes as indigo, opium, marble, tortoise-shell and scent.

Thus in the course of a generation was substituted a chain of off-river wet docks, with ample quays and closely guarded warehouses, for the chaotic conditions in a tidal river in which ships fought for moorings and were involved in constant collisions and groundings while their cargoes lay at the mercy of armies of shore and water thieves. Not only did this transformation enable London and its river, with its vastly increased areas of quay and wharf, to cope with the expansion of ocean trade that followed the Industrial Revolution and Nelson's sea victories but, by providing for the first time bonded warehouses in which imported goods could lie under Customs seal without payment of duty until they were sold, it made London the chief centre of the world's entrepôt trade. This was rendered possible by an Act of Parliament passed in 1803 known as the Warehousing Act, making it lawful for importers of certain dutiable goods, including sugar, tobacco, wine and spirits, to remain 'in bond' in the warehouses of the West India Dock Company and of the London Dock Company, under the joint locks of the Crown and the respective Dock Companies, until such time as the goods were sold and duty became payable.

All this made an immense impression on contemporaries. When in 1814 the Allied Sovereigns visited London—the capital of the country whose wealth and trade, as well as valour, had made their victory over Napoleon possible— among the sights that most aroused their admiration were the new docks of London and their warehouses, piled high with merchandise and treasure from every corner of the earth.

At this time the Port, with its forests of masts in the docks and Pool, its ships constantly passing and repassing, its vast buildings and numerous pleasure resorts and tea-gardens, was one of London's proudest as well as most beautiful sights, and almost every traveller bore witness to it. 'The Custom-House, the Tower, and the Docks,' wrote David Hughson in his *Walks Through London*, 'only form a part of that grand *coup d'œil*, which in a manner extends from Cuckold's Point on the Kentish, and Perry's Wharf on the Essex side of the river. From hence, to the passenger directing his views down the Thames, it may seem like sailing in the midst of a vast inland lake, adorned with shipping of all sizes, and of the construction of almost every nation in the known world . . . Contemplating the riches of the Thames, an elegant poet exclaims:

> And see! by fair Augusta's stately towers,
> Pellucid Thames, his placid current pours:
> To pile her marts contending nations meet,
> The world's productions off'ring at her feet.
> Whate'er of wealth in various regions shines,
> Glows in their sands, or lurks beneath their mines;
> Whate'er from bounteous nature men receive,
> Whatever toil can rear, or art can weave;
> Her princely merchants bear from every zone,
> Their country's stores increasing with their own.'

That, at least, was the theory. A greater poet, viewing the same scene from Shooter's Hill through the eyes of his hero, Don Juan, in 1819 painted a more sombre and realistic picture.

> A mighty mass of brick, and smoke, and shipping,
> Dirty and dusky, but as wide as eye
> Could reach, with here and there a sail just skipping
> In sight, then lost amidst the forestry

Of masts; a wilderness of steeples peeping
On tiptoe through their sea-coal canopy;
A huge, dun cupola, like a foolscap crown
On a fool's head—and there is London Town!

For to all the splendour and display of the magnificent home-terminal of a great Empire's commerce there was a dark reverse—the tall smoking chimneys, now beginning to multiply, along the river's banks, the foul discharges that stained its clear waters, the slums that lurked by the water's edge where daylight never penetrated and fog and vice were endemic.[1]

[1] '*Darkhouse-Lane* the turning immediately joining Billingsgate to the west, contains a number of public-houses, used by watermen, fishermen, females, and others: here, from the confined situation, candles are necessary all day, particularly in winter. As some of these houses are open all night, to accommodate persons waiting for the Gravesend boats, beds may be had for *all*, whether really going to Gravesend, or only pretending so to do. Strangers who act prudently will avoid the mixed company in a place like this, especially such as wish to escape the fangs of those called *kidnappers* or East India crimps.' D. Hughson, *Walks Through London*, 1817, I, 27.

CHAPTER SIX

The Victorian Era

THE new Port system so created served its commercial purpose well during the first half of the nineteenth century. During the second half it proved increasingly inadequate and, in the first years of the present century, was superseded by the Port of London Authority. The nineteenth century in Britain was a period of rapid and revolutionary change, far greater even than that of the eighteenth century. The whole character of national life was revolutionized by scientific and industrial inventions. The size of the largest merchant ship when the Napoleonic War ended in 1815 was around 1,200 tons, and the average well under 500 tons. Eighty years later, at the time of Queen Victoria's Diamond Jubilee, ships of more than 7,000 tons were using the Port, while, with the coming of steam, the length of a voyage to New Zealand had been reduced from four months to eight weeks. The massive docks and warehouses which had been built in the closing years of George III's reign, seemingly for all time, thus became, during the even longer reign of his grand-daughter, antiquated and uneconomic and unable either to support themselves or to serve the Port's expanding needs.

One circumstance, though not in itself the result of social or mechanical change, which made it increasingly difficult for the private Dock Companies to operate was the end of the initial monopoly which they had been given by Parliament. In the Act that created the West India Dock Company it had been laid down that for a period of twenty-one years after the completion of its docks, all vessels arriving in the river from the West Indies must unload and land the whole of their cargoes there. This enabled the Company to recoup its original outlay from the charges and rates it was empowered to levy on tonnage and cargoes. But the spirit of Britain during the nineteenth century was increasingly opposed to monopoly and in favour of freedom of trade, and the Company's monopoly was not renewed. And in the Acts that created it and every other Dock Company a special clause had been inserted called the Free Water Clause, by which freedom from dock charges was granted to all lighters and other river craft engaged in delivering, discharging or receiving ballast or goods to or from sea-going vessels in the private docks. This made the waters of the latter as free as the river itself had been and meant that, from the inception of the docks, cargo could be unloaded into lighters and barges without payment to the dock owners and conveyed to other wharves and quays outside its jurisdiction.

As the ever-growing ocean trade of Victorian England flowed into the river, Victorian individual enterprise was quick to seize every opportunity of profit-making. The private wharfingers and lightermen, with comparatively small capital charges, cashed in on the huge port turnover that the Dock Companies, with their heavy capital expenditure and standing maintenance charges, had made possible. Thus, to combat the competition of those who relied on the Free Water Clause, the Dock Companies were forced to cut their rates and charges, both against their riverside competitors and against one another. This cut-throat competition was intensified by the formation, in that age of eager capital investment, of new Dock Companies with more up-to-date installations which enabled them, too, to undercut and capture the trade of the old. In 1855, during the Crimean War, the Victoria Dock—the first to be linked with the new railways and equipped with rails on its quays—was opened in the hitherto marshy flats below Blackwall, with locks connecting with Bugsby's Reach. Thirteen years later the Millwall Freehold Land and Dock Company followed with the Millwall Docks, built on waste land to the south of the West India Docks and designed to cope with the import of the cheap foreign grain which began to flow into England after the repeal of the Corn Laws and, with far greater rapidity, after the building of the prairie railways. And in 1880 the Royal Albert Dock was opened further down the river opposite Woolwich to accommodate the large steam and iron ships which were taking the place of the wooden sailing vessels of the late Georgian and early Victorian eras. The Tilbury Docks, built by the East and West India Dock Company in the Essex marshlands and opened in 1886— the year before the Queen's Golden Jubilee—were the last of the great docks made by private enterprise. All the while the position of the older Dock Companies was growing steadily worse, for their entrance locks and wharves, built by the Regency capitalists and engineers as though for all time, were unable to accommodate the big steamers which were capturing the cream of the trade with the young countries of the Americas and Antipodes. Even as early as the 'sixties the Wapping dock companies were barely paying their share-holders $3\frac{1}{2}$ per cent—by Victorian standards an impossibly low rate of interest for competitive capital in a business full of risk.

For the dock owners amalgamation was the only remedy. The East India Docks had been taken over by the West India Dock Company in 1838; in 1864 the London and the St. Katharine Dock Companies, which had already merged, were forced to combine with the newly equipped and, therefore, more successful Victoria Dock Company, which in 1880 doubled its facilities for large ships by building the

1¾-mile-long Royal Albert Dock. Meanwhile south of the
river the four companies that had been competing for the
trade of Scandinavia and the Baltic merged, first into two
companies—the Commercial Dock Company and the Grand
Surrey Docks and Canal Company—and, in 1864, into a
single company, the Surrey Commercial Docks Company.
The process of amalgamation was carried still further in
1889 when two of the remaining Dock Companies north of
the river, now scarcely able to meet their expenses, formed
a joint operating committee.

Yet if amalgamation reprieved the private Dock Companies for a time, it completely failed to benefit the worst
sufferers of all from unrestricted *laissez-faire* on the river.
In fact, as the standards of the more humane employers of
labour were reduced to conform to those of the harsher and
less enlightened, it aggravated their condition. As Sir
Joseph Broodbank, the historian of the Port of London, wrote,
'in relation to the public pressure for cheap services it is not
necessarily the competing capitalists who suffer from the
first squeeze of the vice'. To meet the fierce competition that
followed the expiry of the Dock Companies' initial privileges
and the rush for cheap loading contracts under shelter of the
Free Water Clause, reduction of dock labourers' wages had
become almost inevitable. And with the rapid rise in the
population of London and the inflow of poor immigrants
from Ireland and the Continent, cheap labour was readily
available. There followed a terrible deterioration in the
character of dock labour. By the 'fifties the average wage,
when in employment, of the 20,000 labourers in the seven
main London docks was 2s. 4d. a day in winter and 2s. 6d.
in summer, or 4d. an hour, and this for work of the most
exhausting and hazardous kind. But even this pittance was
of the most precarious nature, for owing to the seasonal
character of the river's trade and the uncertain time of

plate vii

LONDON DOCK AT THE CLOSE OF THE NINETEENTH CENTURY

The North Quay and Shipping in the Western Dock about 1896

Photo: Radio Times Hulton Picture Library

plate viii

THE END OF THE ROYAL COMMONWEALTH TOUR, 1954

The arrival of H.M. The Queen and H.R.H. The Duke of Edinburgh in the Royal yacht *Britannia* in the Pool of London, 15 May 1954. The P.L.A. yacht *St. Katharine* is seen in the foreground

Oil painting by Edward Seago, R.B.A. Reproduced by courtesy of Ava, Viscountess Waverley

arrival of ships, most of which were still propelled by sail, dock labour was almost wholly casual. Thus in one week, in 1861, 42 ships berthed in the London docks, in the next 131, in the next 209, and in the next only 29. The effect of this on the life of the dock labourer and his family was terrible; often a man would be without work for weeks at a stretch and in an age when there was no unemployment benefit. 'I've had fourteen shillings a week sometimes', a timber porter, formerly a Dorset farmer's son, told Henry Mayhew, the great social investigator of the mid-Victorian era, 'and many's the week I've had three, and more's the week I've had nothing at all. I've lived on penny loaves, one or two a day when there was no work, and then I've begged.'

Mayhew, writing in the 'fifties, described the scene at the dock gates in the morning when the day's complement of workers was made up.

He who wishes to behold one of the most extraordinary and least-known scenes of this metropolis, should wend his way to the London Dock gates at half-past seven in the morning. There he will see congregated within the principal entrance masses of men of all grades, looks and kinds. Some in half-fashioned surtouts burst at the elbows, with the dirty shirts showing through. Others in greasy sporting jackets, with red pimpled faces. Others in the rags of their half-slang gentility, with the velvet collars of their paletots worn through to the canvas. Some in rusty black, with their waistcoats fastened tight up to the throat. Others, again, with the knowing thieves' curl on each side of the jaunty cap . . . Presently you know, by the stream pouring through the gates and the rush towards particular spots, that the 'calling foremen' have made their appearance. Then begins the scuffling and scrambling forth of countless hands high in the air, to catch the eye of him whose voice may give them work. As the foreman calls from a book the names, some men jump up on the backs of the others, so as to lift themselves high above the rest, and attract the notice of him who hires them. All are shouting. Some cry aloud his surname, some his Christian name, others call out their own names, to remind him that they are there.

D

Now the appeal is made in Irish blarney—now in broken English. Indeed, it is a sight to sadden the most callous, to see thousands of men struggling for only one day's hire; the scuffle being made the fiercer by the knowledge that hundreds out of the number there assembled must be left to idle the day out in want. To look in the faces of that hungry crowd is to see a sight that must be ever remembered. Some are smiling to the foreman to coax him into remembrance of them; others, with their protruding eyes, eager to snatch at the hoped-for pass. For weeks many have gone there, and gone through the same struggle—the same cries; and have gone away, after all, without the work they had screamed for . . . Many of them, it was clear, came to the gate without the means of a day's meal, and, being hired, were obliged to go on credit for the very food they worked upon. What wonder, then, that the calling foreman should be often carried many yards away by the struggle and rush of the men around him seeking employment at his hands! One gentleman assured me that he had been taken off his feet and hurried a distance of a quarter of a mile by the eagerness of the impatient crowd.[1]

'The docks of London', Mayhew continued, 'are to a superficial observer the very focus of metropolitan wealth. The cranes creak with the mass of riches. In the warehouses are stored goods that are as it were ingots of untold gold. Above and below ground you see piles upon piles of treasure that the eye cannot compass. The wealth appears as boundless as the very sea it has traversed. The brain aches in an attempt to comprehend the amount of riches before, above, and beneath it. There are acres upon acres of treasure, more than enough, one would fancy, to stay the cravings of the whole world, and yet you have but to visit the hovels grouped round about all this amazing excess of riches to witness the same amazing excess of poverty. If the incomprehensibility of the wealth rises to sublimity, assuredly the want that co-exists with it is equally incomprehensible and equally sublime. Pass from the quay and warehouses to the courts and alleys that surround them, and the mind is as

[1] Henry Mayhew, *London Labour and the London Poor*, III, 313–15.

bewildered with the destitution of the one place as it is with
the super-abundance of the other. Many come to see the
riches, but few the poverty, abounding in absolute masses
round the far-famed port of London.'

In Gustave Doré's terrible pictures of the docks and East
End in the 'seventies and in the pages of Mayhew one can see
the depths of poverty and degradation to which excessive
competition and a falling labour-market reduced the docker:
the hungry, brutalized men tramping all day, as on a tread-
mill, in wooden wheels that worked the cranes discharging
cargo; the deal porters carrying their immense loads, like
acrobats, as they piled their long, narrow planks over space,
sometimes as many as ninety deals high; the dreadful
accidents of almost daily occurrence when a mangled man or
corpse was carried out through the swarming, shouting
throng. 'Ours is very hard and very dangerous work,' a
docker told Mayhew. 'There is no fund to help or to bury
us, only the parish. In a bad case we're carried to the
Dreadnought or some hospital. If I could have 2s. 6d. a day
for regular work, I'd live twenty years longer than I shall
now, with nothing to do one day and tearing my soul out
with slaving work the others.'

Behind the docks lay the squalid social polity which their
labour conditions helped to create and from which they
drew their workers. Here lay the horror of the Ratcliff
Highway with its perpetual drunken revelry, its brothels,
gambling dens and lodging-houses in which many a poor
sailor shipwrecked, its gangs of thieves and murderers, and
the grim, drab slums which had sprung up to serve the
Port in the marshy, unhealthy land along the river. An East
London magistrate, Montagu Williams, writing in the last
decade of Queen Victoria's reign, when conditions were still
bad enough but many of the worst horrors of the *laissez-faire*
heyday had been mitigated, described the Ratcliff Highway

as it was in the 'sixties, as a 'scene of riots, debaucheries, robberies and all conceivable deeds of darkness . . . From the public-houses there constantly issued the sounds of loud laughter, mingled with shouting and fearful imprecations. Far into the night the women and the drunken sailors danced and sang to the accompaniment of screeching fiddles. If the sailors were not entirely fleeced inside the saloons, the process was completed by bullies and fighting men when they staggered out into the streets.'

But the finest of all descriptions of Victorian dockland comes from the pen of Henry Mayhew. 'As you enter the dock', he wrote of the old London Dock, 'the sight of the forest of masts in the distance, and the tall chimneys vomiting clouds of black smoke, and the many coloured flags flying in the air, has a most peculiar effect; while the sheds with their monster wheels arching through the roofs look like the paddle-boxes of huge steamers. Along the quay you see, now men with their faces blue with indigo, and now gaugers, with their long brass-tipped rules dripping with spirit from the cask they have been probing. Then will come a group of flaxen-haired sailors chattering German; and next a black sailor with a cotton handkerchief twisted turban-like round his head. Presently a blue-smocked butcher, with fresh meat and a bunch of cabbages in the tray on his shoulder; and shortly afterwards a mate, with green paroquets in a wooden cage. Here you will see sitting on a bench a sorrowful-looking woman, with new bright cooking-tins at her feet, telling you she is an emigrant preparing for her voyage. As you pass along this quay the air is pungent with tobacco; on that it overpowers you with the fumes of rum; then you are nearly sickened with the stench of hides and huge bins of horns; and shortly afterwards the atmosphere is fragrant with coffee and spice. Nearly everywhere you meet stacks of cork, or else yellow bins of sulphur or lead-coloured copper ore. As you enter this warehouse, the flooring is sticky, as if it had been newly tarred, with the sugar that has leaked through the casks; and as you descend into the dark vaults, you see long lines of lights hanging from the black arches, and lamps flitting about midway. Here you sniff the fumes of the wine, and there the peculiar fungus-smell of dry rot; then the jumble of sounds as you pass along the dock blends in anything but sweet concord. The sailors are singing boisterous nigger songs from the Yankee ship just entering; the cooper is hammering at the casks on the quay; the chains of the cranes, loosed of their weight, rattle as they fly up again; the ropes splash in the water; some captain shouts his orders through his hands; a goat bleats from some ship in the basin; and empty casks roll along the stones with a heavy drum-like sound. Here the heavily-laden ships are down far below the quay, and you descend to them by ladders; whilst in another basin they are high up out of the water, so that their green copper sheathing is almost level with the eye of the passenger; while above his head a long line of bowsprits stretches far over the quay; and from them hang spars and planks as a gangway to each ship.'

CHAPTER SEVEN

The End of the Companies

URING the 'seventies a reaction set in against the uncontrolled individualism of *laissez-faire* and its calamitous social consequences. It took the form partly of a reforming crusade by middle and upper-class philanthropists to regulate and better the social conditions of the working classes, and partly that of working-class corporate action to obtain better wages. Both these trends— at first limited in their extent but becoming cumulatively stronger as Victoria's reign drew to its close—were reflected in the life of the Port of London. In 1878 the Malvern Mission was founded at Canning Town, out of which grew, through the life work of Reginald Kennedy-Cox, the Dockland Settlements. In 1871 and 1872, shortly after the Commune risings in Paris, the first dockers' strikes took place which resulted in a general rise of wages from the prevailing level of 4*d*. to 5*d*. an hour. These were followed in the late 'eighties, by the far fiercer and more famous struggle for the 'dockers' tanner' with which will always be associated the name of the great working-class orator and agitator, Ben Tillett—first Secretary of the Tea Operatives' and General Labourers' Association. In May 1889 the casual labourers in the East and West India Docks ceased work and marched to the Victoria and London Docks where most of the dock and wharf employees, as well as the lightermen of the private wharfingers, joined them. The strike continued for four months while the entire Port was paralysed and intense public feeling was aroused for the strikers and at the harsh, precarious nature of their lives. In the end, through the intervention of Cardinal Manning, of the Bishop of London and the Lord Mayor, work in the docks was resumed in September, on the basis of a general rise from 5*d*. to 6*d*. an hour on all labour other than piecework, with 8*d*. an hour for overtime.

The great evil of casual labour remained and was indeed temporarily intensified by the general dislocation and ill-feeling caused by the strike. But the Dock Companies agreed that men taken on for the day should henceforward be paid for not less than four hours. And in the following year an important step in the right direction was made by the London and India Docks Joint Committee—now by far the largest employer in the Port. It established in its own docks three grades of privileged labour—a permanent staff entitled to sick pay, annual holidays and pensions after fifteen years' service; registered 'A' labourers employed by the week, with holiday benefits and the right of promotion to the permanent staff when vacancies occurred; and 'B' labourers holding tickets, numbered according to seniority which gave them a first call on casual daily employment when work was available for them.

But the days of the private Dock Companies were now numbered. Prevented by the Free Water Clause and the competition of the wharfingers from offering terms capable of attracting new capital, they were unable to carry out the drastic reconstruction of the Port which the rapid development of ocean shipping made imperative if London was to remain the first port in the world. Liners and merchant vessels alike were growing bigger every year, and deeper and larger docks and a deeper river channel were essential if they were to be accommodated in the Thames. The principal shipowners using the river were now demanding a channel to the Royal Docks thirty feet deep at low water, and the

plate ix   THE PORT OF LONDON AUTHORITY HEADQUARTERS, TOWER HILL, LONDON, 1925

Etching by Kenneth Ames   Collection of the Port of London Authority

plate x

BREAKWATER CAISSONS FOR THE 'MULBERRY' INVASION HARBOURS, 1944

Under construction in East India (Import) Dock, 1944 *Chalk and wash drawing by Sir Muirhead Bone*

Reproduced by courtesy of the Trustees of the Imperial War Museum

plate xi   ONE OF THE COMPLETELY MECHANIZED EXPORT BERTHS IN THE PORT OF LONDON, 1958

A busy scene showing the up-to-date mechanical equipment at Nos. 25/27 sheds, Royal Albert Dock   *Photo: P.L.A.*

plate xii

ROYAL VICTORIA DOCK, 1948

Oil painting by A. J. W. Burgess, R.I., R.O.I. (1879–1957)   Collection of the Port of London Authority

Thames Conservancy Board—the public authority created
in 1857 and charged with the duty of maintaining the river
channel—though it did its best felt itself unable to dredge
to a depth sufficient to satisfy them. Meanwhile John Burns,
the working-class leader who, with Ben Tillett, had played
the leading part in the Dockers' Strike of 1889, and inci-
dentally was a keen student of London history, was advo-
cating a return, under reformed conditions, to the traditional
system under which London's port and river were administered by the public body elected by its citizens, in this case
to be, not the Corporation of the old City, but the new
London County Council.

It was not, however, a Municipal or Socialist solution that
was to provide the remedy for the growing problems of the
Port, though it came at a time when municipal formulas for
reforming society were beginning to be fashionable. In the
last year of the old century, driven to despair by the diversion
from their half-empty wharves and warehouses of cargoes
unloaded into the lighters of competitors protected by the
Free Water Clause, the Dock Companies petitioned
Parliament for a licence to levy charges on all craft using
their waters. This proposal for a new monopoly met with the
fiercest hostility and the Bill they presented failed. But the
ventilation of their financial plight drew widespread attention
to the needs of the Port, and in 1900, as a century earlier,
a Commission was set up 'to inquire into the present administration of the Port of London and the water approaches
thereto'. When in 1902 this Royal Commission on the Port
of London issued its Report—in the summer of Edward VII's
Coronation—it was to recommend the creation of an entirely
new kind of Port Authority representing all who used the Port.

So came about the genesis of the Port of London Authority.
It was the Liberal Government of 1906, with its vast
majority and strong reforming impulse, which undertook

the task of devising and carrying through Parliament the measures to give the Commission's recommendations effect. The successive Presidents of the Board of Trade who introduced the First and Second Readings of the Port of London Bill were the two members of the Government whose names were to go down to history among Britain's very greatest—David Lloyd George and Winston Churchill. The Parliamentary Secretary who steered the Bill through the Commons was 52-year-old Sir Hudson Ewbanke Kearley, a successful business man who so identified himself with the measure that he was nominated by the Government as the Port of London Authority's first Chairman.

The Authority was to be a self-governing public trust— an Edwardian and typically British compromise between the Regency and Victorian ideal of unrestricted private enterprise and the still untried twentieth-century Socialist ideal of untrammelled public ownership. Created by the Port of London Act, which received the Royal Assent on 21 December 1908, it was to consist of twenty-eight members, ten of them representing public authorities and eighteen elected by the private users of the Port—shipowners, merchants, wharfingers and owners of river craft—with a Chairman and Vice-Chairman whom its members were to be free, if they chose, to elect from outside. The nominated members were to be appointed, four by the London County Council, two by the City Corporation, two by the Board of Trade, one by the Admiralty and one by Trinity House. The Authority was not given a complete monopoly, for Trinity House retained its ancient jurisdiction over pilotage, buoying and lighting, and the City Corporation its sanitary supervision of shipping, passengers and cargo. The Metropolitan Police, too, continued to exercise patrol of the tideway, though not of the docks which were to be policed, like the private docks before them, by the Authority's own police force. And the time-honoured Free Water Clause continued to operate, though with two important reservations—the payment of a registration fee by all barges using the Port, and the Authority's right, though this has never been exercised, to acquire by compulsory purchase, if necessary, all private wharves and warehouses along the river.

Subject to these exceptions the Authority took over from the Dock Companies on 31 March 1909 the entire ownership and control of the 2,700-acre estate containing the docks, and from the Thames Conservancy Board the control of the sixty-nine miles of tidal river from Teddington to the sea. It was given statutory powers to levy port rates on all goods, and tonnage dues on all ships entering the docks and to charge for storage and services in its warehouses. It was empowered to raise capital from the public of up to, at the start, £27 millions, in the form of fixed-interest-bearing stock. Any excess of revenue over expenditure, after payment of interest, was to be used for port improvements, new equipment and the reduction of port dues and charges. It was, in short, to serve the public on a basis of charging for services rendered but without the object of private gain.

In his opening address the Chairman—Lord Devonport as he shortly afterwards became—defined the Authority's aims. It was not, he said, 'to create a new business, inasmuch as we succeed a series of undertakings long in existence that must be carried on without interruption for a single moment . . . Our great and initial responsibility will be to weld them into one control and management . . . The benefit will not be for the London of today or tomorrow, but we shall have laid the foundation of an enduring prosperity that will continue far into and enrich the future.'

CHAPTER EIGHT

The Port of London Authority

IN this prophetic and constructive spirit, the new Authority, putting first things first, began at once on a work of immense magnitude—the dredging of fifty million tons of spoil from the river bed to create the longest deep-water channel in the world, enabling ships of 6,000 tons to reach the Pool of London, and vessels of up to 35,000 tons to berth in the Royal group of docks at North Woolwich, within six miles of the heart of the City. Simultaneously the P.L.A., as it became called, set to work to weld the five dock groups of the Port, all previously developed on different lines, into a single whole, serving in the most effective and economical way possible the needs of those using the Port—a task which in the nature of things was bound to take many years. New quays and sheds, cranes and pumping installations, enlarged dock entrances to allow for changes and developments—the point on which the late nineteenth century Dock Companies had failed—a cargo jetty at Tilbury, additional cold-storage accommodation and a new chilled-meat berth, and a fitting Head Office for the Authority on Tower Hill were all part of the programme set forth by Lord Devonport and carried out with unswerving purpose and efficiency.

A man of so much drive and determination was bound to arouse opposition in the course of his work. In the second year of the Authority's life it became involved in a major industrial dispute with the new National Transport Workers' Federation, formed in 1910 by the amalgamation of the

country's various dock and transport Trade Unions. In
1911 this body approached the P.L.A. with a demand for
improved conditions of pay and employment. As a result of
a conference presided over by Lord Devonport and attended
by all the principal shipowners and wharfingers using the
Port, an agreement was reached, known as the Devonport
Agreement, by which the dockers' day rate was to be raised
from 6*d*. to 7*d*. an hour and overtime from 8*d*. to 9*d*., while
the hours of day labour, hitherto from 6 a.m. to 6 p.m., were
reduced by an hour. But for some reason which was never
clear the agreement, though reached in a spirit of remarkable
amity, was almost immediately repudiated by the Transport
Federation's leaders who demanded a further penny an
hour. This Lord Devonport regarded as a breach of faith. He
accordingly refused to negotiate further with them or, when
the Union leaders called their members out, to yield an inch.
He would, he declared, starve the men into submission
rather than compromise. In the strikes of that August—one
of the hottest of the century—and of the following summer
such bitterness was aroused that on one occasion the veteran
Trade Union leader, Ben Tillett, led a vast concourse of
dockers on Tower Hill in the prayer, 'Oh God! strike Lord
Devonport dead!'[1]

The strikes failed and the men went back to work on the
basis of the original Devonport Agreement. Nor was the
Union's attempt to enforce the 'closed shop' in the docks
successful. Lord Devonport's inflexible will prevailed. But
the conflict left behind a legacy of great bitterness. Across
these unhappy divisions and across the constructive work of
the P.L.A. alike, broke in 1914 the First World War. During
it, while retaining his position as Chairman of the Authority,

[1] It should be remembered, however, that this incident occurred in the
heat of the moment and that at the time of Lord Devonport's death in
1934 he and Ben Tillett, on the latter's testimony, were good friends.

Lord Devonport became for a time the nation's first Food Controller, leaving on the public, as he had done on the dockers, the impact of his strong authoritarian character but bringing to his task the same single-minded devotion to duty.

For Viscount Devonport, as he became in 1917, and the P.L.A., the war was a tragic interruption to the long-term work of reconstructing the Port. For four years it was laid aside, only to be resumed with the same vigour as soon as the war was over. In 1920, two years after the Armistice, the new Cold Air Stores at the Royal Albert Dock were completed, and in the following year, accompanied by the Queen, King George V opened the great new dock that was to bear his name at North Woolwich, the most up-to-date in the world at that time and capable of accommodating vessels of up to 35,000 tons. In his speech the King, himself a sailor, spoke of the Port—'in which Chaucer worked as a Custom House official and Drake, the founder of our sea power, entertained his sovereign on board the *Golden Hind*'—as 'deeply interwoven with the fabric of English history'. A year later, in 1922, the Prime Minister, David Lloyd George, opened the P.L.A.'s new Headquarters Building on Tower Hill, on the very site of the house where Peter the Great lived when he came to England to learn shipbuilding, and a stone's throw from the site of the Navy Office, where the greatest of Britain's naval administrators, Samuel Pepys, did his work.

In 1925 Lord Devonport retired and was succeeded by Lord Ritchie of Dundee. During his fifteen years of office more than eighty acres of dock water and six miles of quay had been added to the Port, while the fifty-mile dredged channel from the sea to London Bridge, 1,000 feet wide and 30 feet deep at mean low water in its lower reaches, was now nearing completion. It has been calculated that the spoil excavated to make this magnificent water highway was sufficient to form a mountain half as high as Snowdon.

In 1926—the year that saw the opening of the new deep-water Quebec Dock at Rotherhithe—the work of reconstructing the Port was interrupted by the General Strike, during which the P.L.A., with the help of volunteer and naval labour, contrived to keep London—public and strikers alike—fed and supplied. There is a charming story, told by the late Lord Halifax, of how during its course, when the gates outside the docks were besieged by angry crowds of strikers and their relations, and laden lorries from time to time emerged, either guarded by soldiers with steel helmets or bearing large printed notices inscribed, 'Acting under the authority of the T.U.C.', there issued—to be greeted, after a moment of astonished silence by prolonged cheering and laughter—a vegetable cart drawn by a donkey and driven by an elderly gentleman in a very dented bowler hat bearing the inscription, 'Acting under the authority of my own bloody self!'

The advantage of entrusting the Port's development to a Public Trust, run by practical men of business and proved experience, was shown during the period of depression, mass unemployment and checkered recovery that followed the First World War. The Authority refused to be deterred from its long-term constructive plans and persisted in carrying out the work to which it had set its hand. By doing so it helped to alleviate the shortage of employment and purchasing power in London. New timber sheds were built and new discharging berths in the development of Lavender and Acorn Ponds at the Surrey Commercial Docks in 1928 to serve the Canadian, Scandinavian and Russian softwood trade. Old docks like the West India Import and Export Docks and the South West India and Millwall Docks were joined by cuttings and given improved entrances from the river, and at Tilbury were built a vast new dry dock, 750 feet long, the New Entrance Lock 1,000 feet long and a

plate xiii

TILBURY OCEAN CARGO AND PASSENGER TERMINAL, 1957
The largest ocean-going liners using the Port of London can be accommodated at the new No. 1 Berth at Tilbury Docks *Photo: P.L.A.*

plate xiv

THE NEW NO. 4 BERTH AT ROYAL VICTORIA DOCK, 1960

The last available area in Royal Victoria Dock is here seen developed by the construction of a berth, for two ships, 1,290 feet long, for the American trade. In fifty years the Authority has redeveloped the entire dock

Photo by courtesy of Tubewrights Limited

Passenger Landing Stage capable of disembarking passengers from the largest liners. And despite much suspicion and opposition by organized Labour, the first steps were taken to re-equip the docks with mechanical installations, including a self-propelled floating crane of 150 tons which was christened the 'London Mammoth'. Not, however, until the effects of the world economic depression which followed the collapse of the American Stock market in 1929 and the financial crisis of 1931 in this country had been in part overcome was the Authority able to proceed with its full development schemes. Commencing in 1936 the old jetties of the Royal Victoria Dock were swept away and by 1939 had been replaced by a three-quarter-mile lineal deep-water quay. Plans were also put in hand for deepening both the Royal Victoria and the Royal Albert Docks. Meanwhile to meet the requirements of the country's fast developing road transport, a wide two-mile approach-road to the docks was built by the Ministry of Transport called Silvertown Way. At the same time, as an act of faith and courage, the Authority reduced its port charges to draw new custom to the river, thus continuing in times of slump the process it had begun in prosperity. In the twelve years between 1925 and the end of 1936 the Authority reduced the annual charges of the Port by more than a million pounds.

The reward of all this activity was that by the time the P.L.A. celebrated its thirtieth birthday on the eve of the Second World War, the total tonnage using the Port had grown from under forty million to over sixty million net registered tons, while the annual value of its imports and exports—£322 million in 1909—was almost half as much again. During the same period the percentage of the United Kingdom's seaborne trade handled in the Port had risen from twenty-nine per cent to nearly thirty-eight per cent. Thanks to the Authority's work London had recovered, and more than recovered, its ancient place of unchallenged maritime pre-eminence.

E

CHAPTER NINE

The Second World War

IN 1939 came the tragedy of the Second World War. No major institution in the country was harder hit by what followed than the Port of London. Even during the opening months of the so-called 'phoney-war' winter, the Thames estuary was besieged with magnetic mines which threatened at one moment—till the crisis had been heroically met and overcome—to bring the life of the Port to a standstill. And when in the summer of 1940 the war on the Continent began in earnest, the river craft of London and the personnel of the P.L.A. played a priceless part in the evacuation of Britain's imperilled army from Dunkirk. Among the ships from the river that crossed the North Sea and sailed into the inferno were spritsail barges, tugs, yachts, shrimping bawleys, a fire-float, a sludge-hopper, and more than eight hundred Thames life-boats. A few of their impromptu crews, briefed in the P.L.A.'s offices, embarked wearing bowler hats and armed with umbrellas.

But the full shock of modern war did not fall on the Port until the great aerial bombardments of London began in September 1940. Then indeed it was in the front-line of war and bore the full brunt. Late in the afternoon of Saturday 7 September—a lovely summer day—four hundred of Goering's bombers struck at the docks as the first blow of what was intended to be the knock-out for London and the British Empire. It was designed as the English 'Rotterdam'. All the docks with the exception of Tilbury suffered immense damage, and the timber storage yards of the Surrey

Commercial Docks were set ablaze from end to end, burning
for nearly a week. That night, guided by the greatest
conflagration seen in London since the Fire of 1666, a further
fleet of bombers rained destruction on the Port and the
crowded dwellings of Dockland. Sir Alan Herbert has left
us a wonderful description of the river that night. After
watching four piers burning simultaneously in Limehouse
Reach, he was ordered as a Petty Officer of the Royal Naval
Patrol Service to find a P.L.A. wreck-lighter in the Lower
Pool, to pick up some wire from her and to take it down to
Woolwich where it was urgently needed for towing burning
barges.

We rounded Limehouse Corner and saw an astounding picture.
Half a mile of the Surrey shore, ending before the Greenland
Entrance of the Surrey Commercial Docks, was ablaze—warehouses,
wharves, piers, dolphins, barges. The wind was westerly, and there
was a wall of smoke and sparks across the river. Burning barges were
drifting everywhere, and I thought, 'Well, this is surely where they
want our wire'. But there was not a soul in sight—the small police-
boat ahead of us had turned back to report—and we had been
ordered to Woolwich. A wooden ship, and petrol-driven, we did not
like the look of it much: but we put wet towels round our faces and
steamed at half-speed into the torrid cloud. Inside, the scene was
like a lake in Hell.[1]

For fifty-seven consecutive nights the docks and river
were under bombardment and the employees of the Authority in continuous action. Its Headquarters Building received
a direct hit on the night of 8 December 1940, the central
Rotunda crashing to the ground. Head Office had a second
direct hit during the night of 10 May 1941. There were
nights when it seemed as if the river itself were on fire. On
25 September 1940, lying by the old *Seven Seas* schooner at
Charing Cross, Alan Herbert awoke to see the signal box on
Hungerford Bridge blazing overhead and Waterloo Bridge,

[1] A. P. Herbert, *Independent Member*, 1950. 169–70.

still encased in scaffolding, on fire too. 'Day by day', he wrote, 'as the blitz roared on, we saw the wounds of London River from top to bottom—the wreck of a tug in Northfleet Hope, a big hole in Tilbury Landing Stage, a big bite out of the jetty at Barking Power Station, oil-tanks blazing at Purfleet, the shattered "skid" astern of a mine-sweeper that meant a mine had gone up, a collier sunk off Beckton Gas-works, another pub gone west off Blackwall, two new green "wreck" flags opposite Greenwich, suspicious smoke from Ford's works at Dagenham, a train hit at Cannon Street Bridge, the Tower Bridge not working today.'[1]

Not till 3 November did London and London River have a night without bombs. And even in November, more than two months after the blitz started, there were only three nights without a raid.

Throughout the war, though still served by its ordinary peacetime Members and a greatly diminished staff, the Port of London Authority operated as a Port Emergency Committee responsible to the Ministry of Transport and with increased powers. Its attitude to its emergency duties was epitomized in a speech made on the outbreak of war by the Chairman of the River Emergency Committee, Mr. W. L. Wrightson,

The Port, however fiercely attacked, is indestructible. We are ready; we are prepared to carry on, whatever may happen; and we are satisfied that whatever calls may be made on us or on our officers and staff, they will be acted upon and fulfilled with the utmost efficiency.

Among the Emergency Committee's duties were the civil defence of the docks and river, the provision of fire-fighting, gas-cleansing and first-aid stations, and the removal to safe storage areas inland and their subsequent maintenance of huge quantities of foodstuffs and raw materials normally

[1] *Idem*, 167–68.

housed in the docks. Through all the minings and blitzes of those exacting years it maintained salvage and wreck-raising services for the entire Thames estuary and assisted the Admiralty in a ceaseless war against the enemy's attempts—by bomber, minelayer, E-boat, submarine, long-range gun, flying bomb and rocket—to sink or immobilize the ships that carried London's food and raw materials. Thousands of volunteers kept nightly watch on its sixty miles of tideway and anything that fell in its waters was immediately reported to the Flag-Officer-in-Charge, London, at his headquarters in the Port of London Building, Tower Hill, and transmitted by him for action to his mine-sweeping and clearance sections.

During the latter stages of the war, though more than four million tons of the shipping that normally used the Port had been sunk on the high seas and London's seaborne commerce was reduced to a quarter of its peacetime volume —partly on account of the deliberate diversion of shipping from London—the Port played a major part in the prepara-tions for the greatest amphibious military operation in history. The larger portion of the huge prefabricated artificial harbours which later, in the wake of Montgomery's and Bradley's armies, were towed from the Thames to the South Coast and thence, on D-Day, to Normandy, were secretly built in the Port of London. So was the 'Pluto' pipe-line that supplied the Liberation Armies with fuel and made their break-out and rapid advance possible. On D-Day more than three hundred London ships and a thousand barges sailed from the Port, carrying 50,000 soldiers, 9,000 vehicles and nearly 80,000 tons of military supplies. In all, between June 1944 and the end of the war in Europe, 2,760,000 tons of military stores, including more than 200,000 vehicles, were shipped to the battlefields from the Thames. When in the spring of 1944 General Montgomery told an audience of 16,000 London dock workers that on their efforts in the coming months the success or failure of the attempt to free the Continent would depend, he was stating what, in the light of what happened, proved to be an unchallengeable historical fact.

CHAPTER TEN

A Port Re-born

W HEN the war ended those who administered the Port were faced by a Herculean task. Nearly a thousand high-explosive missiles and thousands of incendiary bombs had fallen on its property—the most consistently and heavily bombed civilian target in the British Isles. One-third of its warehouses and transit sheds had been destroyed or damaged, and half its total storage accommodation. The P.L.A.'s financial loss in terms of 1939 values was assessed by the War Damage Commission at thirteen and a half million pounds. With much of its equipment removed during the war by the Services or transferred to other ports at home and abroad, and most of what remained in need of repair, with much of the shipping that was its peacetime life-blood sunk or deflected to other purposes, and with the river itself threatening to silt up for lack of six years' dredging, the P.L.A. had to restore its house with broken tools. It was confronted by stringent Government restrictions on the use of materials, labour and capital and by the general national weariness that inevitably followed in the wake of war.

Yet never in Britain's history had seaborne commerce been more essential for her survival. With her pre-war savings gone, her existence depended almost wholly on her export trade. Fortunately, in the hour of the Port's greatest need, the man to meet it was at hand. On 3 January 1946, Sir John Anderson was appointed Chairman of the P.L.A. and six years later became Viscount Waverley of Westdean. The outstanding Civil Servant of his generation, with a record of brilliant success in half a dozen different fields, he had won public fame in the 'thirties by the calm and courage with which he had faced assassination while governing an Indian province. Then in the years immediately before the war he had entered politics to become, in the course of a decade, Lord Privy Seal, Home Secretary, Lord President of the Council, Chancellor of the Exchequer and a member of Churchill's War Cabinet. Now, at the age of sixty-three, he returned to his first love, administration. In this he had few equals and no superiors. With his incisive mind, massive presence and, under that grave dignity which the ancients called *gravitas*, a profound humanity and understanding of his fellow men, this calm, wise, courageous Scot, with the immense prestige and fund of goodwill which his character and career had won for him, was perfectly fitted to deal with the exigencies of the time. Expecting of every man the best of which he was capable yet never blaming anyone for inability to do more than his best and himself incapable of injustice, he won from all who worked with him the highest measure of efficiency and loyalty. Resolute, imperturbable and immensely able, of all the great men who have served the Port he was perhaps the greatest.

The work of the P.L.A. during the first few years after the war was largely to make good its losses, particularly of its storage accommodation of which it had lost approximately fifty per cent. During hostilities the greatest warehousing port in the world had recourse to prefabricated huts erected among the ruins of burnt-out warehouses for the safe storage of its cargoes; some even remained in the open under tarpaulins. One of the Authority's first tasks was the salvage or dispersal of the wrecks remaining in the Lower River and estuary. Altogether during the war and subsequently the P.L.A. raised 35 ships and 600 small craft and dispersed the wrecks of 8 ships.

It was imperative that if London was to play an effective part in post-war economy and in the export drive an intense effort must be made to accelerate the rehabilitation of the Port and in 1948 the present General Manager, now Sir Leslie Ford, was appointed to direct this effort.

As the shortages of labour, materials and finance gradually eased, the outline began to take shape of a new Port of London, or rather an ancient port reborn after calamity to meet the commercial requirements of the second half of the twentieth century. The first need was equipment to turn the immensely expensive ships of today round quickly and so reduce maintenance and docking costs. This involved an increased use of every kind of cargo-handling machine, both on the dockside and in the warehouse. Here the experiences of war proved invaluable, and advantage was taken of the advances in machine design made under stress of military necessity.

Many of these were of the most revolutionary kind. The greatest care had to be taken, however, to meet the very real fears of the dock labourers and their Unions. Only by the most delicate and cautious approach was it possible to overcome the intense suspicion felt for labour-saving machinery by those who had known mass unemployment in the 'twenties and 'thirties and who instinctively viewed new mechanized aids to labour as a mere means for reducing the wage-bill.

To achieve this the P.L.A. first made, in the words of the General Manager, 'a preliminary study of the efficient and economical implementation of mechanical handling into work processes'. One of the objectives in planning new cargo-handling-and-storing machinery was to achieve the maximum efficiency through working uniformity in the shape, size and weight of the packages handled. But this, for port and ship operating work, involved far more complex

calculations and considerations than the mechanical moving
of goods in unit-load form on land. It necessitated explora-
tory discussions with a wide variety of clients and customers:
shipowners, manufacturers, H.M. Customs authorities,
wharfingers and, above all, Trade Union officials. To meet
the susceptibilities of Labour and convince its representatives that mechanization, rightly applied, instead of worsen-
ing security and conditions of employment would strengthen
and improve them, and to study and master the peculiar
problems of conveying packaged loads to and from ship by
machinery, a pilot scheme was launched in 1951 at a specially
designed loading-berth at the West India Dock. The result
was a triumph for the Authority's planners. Cargo for
export was unloaded from road and rail direct to 3-ton
dock-tool pallets, conveyed on them by fork-lift trucks to
sheds with easy access, level hard-wearing floors and high
roofing. There it was piled four loads high, to port-marks,
and from thence was later transferred by the same mechanical means and by crane to the ship's hold, the pallets then
being returned to the quay. The speed of shiploading was
increased by more than twenty per cent and the number of
manhandling operations in the process reduced from five to
two. Yet the greater efficiency and economy in loading
achieved so increased the volume of trade passing through
the dock that it assured both higher wages and more continuous employment for the loading gangs, as well as the
elimination of much of the hard manual work and danger
hitherto inseparable from the docker's life.

This highly successful experiment served as a prototype
for mechanized berths and new types of transit sheds not
only at the West India Docks but at the Royal Albert Dock
and the Surrey Commercial Docks. During the early 'fifties
'standard' fork-lift trucks and pallets and mobile cranes and
electric quay-cranes were installed in all the five dock

groups, and, to quote Sir Leslie Ford, 'a new rhythm of mechanized cargo handling began to take the place of methods conceived in an age of unlimited manual labour'. Two main principles were applied in rebuilding the quays and transit sheds; access by water, road and rail was rendered as simple and extensive as possible, and the roofs and doors of all buildings were made high and wide enough to allow mobile cranes and fork-lift trucks to enter, stack and pile goods in every part of the interior, while upright supports were, wherever possible, avoided to allow of maximum manœuvring space.

This transformation of dock processes, which is turning the docker from a manual labourer doing the hardest chores into a highly skilled technician handling intricate and costly machinery, has been greatly facilitated by the creation by the Government during the war—largely at the instance of that great champion of the docker, the late Ernest Bevin, when Minister of Labour and National Service—of a National Dock Labour Corporation, to register and pay a basic weekly wage to all dock workers not on the regular staff of the P.L.A. or of some other port employer. In 1947 this wartime body's functions were taken over by the National Dock Labour Board, which by guaranteeing all registered dock workers a weekly minimum wage with attendance money and paid holidays, raised the status and conditions of the casual dock labourer to a level undreamed of by the social reformers and Trade Union pioneers of the late Victorian era. A wartime innovation by the P.L.A. which much improved conditions for dock labour was the dock canteen. Introduced voluntarily by the Authority during the 1940 blitz to feed men deprived by bombing of their eating, refreshment and public houses, it was given statutory recognition by the Docks (Provision of Canteens) Act of 1941 which authorized and required the P.L.A. to provide canteen accommodation and hot meals not only for its own employees but for all workers in docks. Today the Authority operates forty permanent canteens and serves 6,000 mid-day meals a day, as well as some 14,000 snacks and 18,000 cups of tea, in premises and under conditions which are rightly regarded as a model of hygienic catering.

In its work of post-war reconstruction the P.L.A. has spent more than 30 million pounds on maintenance and 3 million pounds more on the purchase of mechanical equipment. It has restored and improved the tideway, which is now operated in three sectors and patrolled day and night by the diesel launches of its new Thames Navigation Service which, fitted with radar and radio telephone, are in round-the-clock touch with a central Information and Communications Centre at Gravesend, where all essential information is recorded and prepared for transmission to ships on frequencies allocated in accordance with the International Maritime V.H.F. Agreement. The Authority has also carried out in recent years an intensive technical research into the regimen of the River Thames by means of a large-scale hydraulic model in order to ascertain the causes of siltation and the best means of controlling and reducing it. All this has made an immense contribution to the safety of shipping, especially in fog and bad weather, and to the ease of navigation.

With every year that passes the P.L.A.'s equipment and technical resources are expanding to meet the needs of our age of advanced technology. In its half-century of existence the net register tonnage of the traffic handled in the Port has more than doubled. One-fifth of the shipping tonnage of the United Kingdom passes through the Port, carrying goods to the value of one-third of the total United Kingdom's imports and exports. Every week over a thousand vessels enter and leave the Thames, and in the year preceding the

P.L.A.'s Jubilee—when, following Lord Waverley's death, its Chairmanship passed to Viscount Simon—more than 57,000 ships used the Port. Today, fifty years after its foundation and with its work of post-war reconstruction almost completed, the Authority operates the largest single dock area in the world with five great dock systems, thirty-six miles of deep-water quays and warehousing accommodation and services unrivalled by any other port. With an astonishing range of craftsmen and technicians of every kind and its own police force, it employs a permanent staff of more than 10,000. About forty-six per cent of the shipping using the Port enters and leaves the wet-dock premises of the P.L.A., whilst approximately fourteen per cent of the total volume of goods passing through the Port—more than 52,000,000 tons in 1959—passes over the quays of the Authority, the balance being dealt with overside either in the river or in the docks or at private wharves. During the year ending 31 March 1910 the Authority handled 2,636,621 tons of imports and exports. By 1959 the figure had risen to 4,140,464 tons.

This great public corporation serves the needs, not only of importers and exporters, shippers and shipowners who directly use and pay for its facilities, but of numerous riverside wharves and wharfingers who are both its customers and competitors. It is the Authority's pride that it is not a monopoly but represents all the users of the Port, both private and statutory—a public trust offering public service in an economy based on free enterprise. Most of the 7,000 tugs and barges that work in the Port and river are privately owned. And the Authority works in harness with other Public Authorities; with the Corporation of Trinity House whose pilots still exercise the exclusive right to bring sea-going ships up the river; with the National Dock Labour Board which supplies dock labour for all work that cannot be performed by permanent employees; with H.M. Customs and Excise, and the Immigration Officers of the Home Office; with the Thames Division of the Metropolitan Police and the Kent and Essex County Constabularies; with the Medical Officer of Health of the City of London; and with the various Local Authorities and Utility Corporations who provide and maintain bridges, ferries and tunnels across or under its waters.

plate xv AN AERIAL VIEW OF THE ROYAL VICTORIA, THE ROYAL ALBERT AND THE KING GEORGE V DOCKS, 1960

The intense concentration of ocean-going ships on a busy day at the three Royal Docks cannot be rivalled anywhere else in the world. The view looking westward shows every berth occupied in a total length of quayage measuring over eleven miles   *Photo: Aerofilms Limited*

plate xvi

THE PORT OF LONDON AUTHORITY'S JUBILEE CELEBRATIONS, 1959

Her Majesty The Queen and Prince Philip visited the Head Office and the Docks of the Authority on 12 May 1959 and they had a wonderful reception from thousands of dock workers. Here they are seen in the Royal Albert Dock at No. 35 Berth escorted by Viscount Simon, Chairman of the Authority, Lord Cottesloe, Vice-Chairman and Sir Leslie Ford, General Manager. Mr. G. T. Johnson, the Dock Superintendent, is presenting members of the staff. *Photo: News Chronicle*

CHAPTER ELEVEN

The Docks Today

WHOEVER approaches London from the sea comes upon the first of the Authority's dock groups at Tilbury, twenty-six miles below London Bridge. Here, flanked by a lockside garden—for long the first sight of English soil to greet the home-coming voyager—is the entrance lock to the 106 acres of enclosed docks where the greatest liners lie between their ocean voyages. These docks have been greatly increased in size since they were taken over by the P.L.A. in 1909. Here are twenty-one deep-water berths and four miles of built-up quay where ships of up to 30,000 tons lie, and no less than three dry docks, the latest built equipped with hydraulically operated bilge-blocks and a leading-in girder which automatically centralizes the bows of any vessel entering it. Here, too, along the riverside to the south of the docks, is the 1,000-feet-long, double-deck cargo-jetty built by the Authority during and after the First World War to enable ships to load or discharge without entering the docks and where today some 6,000 tons of latex are pumped annually from ships lying alongside into storage tanks on land leased by the Authority. The jetty lies 160 feet from the Essex shore and is connected by a viaduct with the dock railway system, which serves the thirty-four transit sheds built along the quays of the docks.

The crowning glories of Tilbury are the great 1,142-feet-long floating Passenger Landing Stage, in the river, built by the P.L.A. in 1930, in conjunction with the new Riverside Station built by the L.M.S. Railway, and the new Ocean

F

Passenger Terminal which the Authority constructed and opened in Tilbury Docks in 1957 at a cost of £1,590,000. Designed to meet the expanding needs of the future, the latter has a T-shaped transit shed 100,000 feet square, a Baggage Hall and a magnificent Reception Hall decorated with black and white murals and a statue of St. Christopher, the patron saint of travellers. Here are all the facilities needed by passengers—nearly a quarter of a million of whom pass through the Port annually: banking, communications and refreshment services, a viewing gallery for waiting friends and relations overlooking the quay, a railway station served by boat-trains from St. Pancras, and a covered car-park with a public-address system, twenty pick-up points and accommodation for seven hundred vehicles. Road transport using Tilbury has increased enormously in recent years— seventy per cent of the cargo landed today is removed by road compared with twelve per cent before the war—and the Authority has built nearly two miles of roads within the docks and three vehicle parks which, already served by arterial approach-roads, will soon be linked both with a new Trunk Road to the north and the all but completed Dartford– Purfleet tunnel to the south. Tilbury Docks have transit facilities only, with no warehouses for long storage, though some cargo is delivered by rail for housing at the Commercial Road Warehouse. The principal imports of Tilbury Docks, tea and wool, are delivered overside to be lightered up to London Dock for warehousing.

*   *   *

The next of the P.L.A.'s great dock systems is fifteen miles higher up the river. Here at North Woolwich, forty miles from the open sea, with its three entrances leading out of Gallions Reach, are the 234 inter-connected acres of water of the Royal Victoria, Royal Albert and King George V Docks, colloquially known as the Royal Docks, together constituting the largest sheet of impounded dock water in the world. In the Royal Victoria Dock, now modernized out of recognition and the most up-to-date in equipment of all the P.L.A.'s docks, is the centre of the tobacco trade in the Port, where warehouses, equipped with overhead travelling cranes, afford unrivalled facilities for garbling, sampling and other technical operations carried out by the Authority's warehouse staff on behalf of the tobacco importers who keep their wares in bond here. Here, too, are mechanized berths for the discharge and delivery of South American chilled beef, and specially designed and equipped sheds for the handling of green fruit and vegetables. And on the south side of this great eighty-six-acre dock are the Authority's silos for the storage of grain, and four large private flour-mills, into which grain in bulk can be discharged from ships alongside by pneumatic suction-plant. Seven floating pneumatic grain-elevators, each capable of discharging 300 tons per hour, are based here at the Bulk Grain Department. They are used not only in this dock system but also in the India and Millwall and the Surrey Commercial Docks.

The Royal Albert Dock, lying to the east of the Royal Victoria Dock and giving access to it, is the headquarters of London's frozen meat trade and is furnished with three cold-air stores built during the First World War. The Authority provides accommodation and equipment for inspecting, cutting and glanding meat, employs a highly skilled staff for carrying out such duties, and operates two subsidiary stores at Smithfield Market to which meat can be sent from the docks by insulated van ready for immediate sale. Altogether, there is accommodation in the P.L.A.'s cold-air stores for over half a million carcasses. Another facility offered by the Royal Albert Dock is a mechanized berth for the discharge of bananas, capable of unloading and despatching more than 80,000 stems in a day.

F*

The third dock in this immense trinity of impounded water, quays, transit sheds and warehouses, is the King George V Dock—the only one of the major docks to have been built by the Authority and which was opened by H.M. King George V on 8 July 1921. It has a depth of thirty-eight feet with an entrance lock from Gallions Reach 100 feet wide and 800 feet long, through which in 1939 the 35,655-ton *Mauretania* was able to pass when she berthed in the Royal Docks. The North Quay of this superb modern dock is equipped with six two-storeyed warehouses with a total area of more than 700,000 square feet, and is served by two lines of railway on the quayside and three lines of railway at the back of the warehouses, as well as twenty-seven electric cranes with a carrying capacity of up to five tons. Cargo is conveyed to the upper floors of the warehouses by crane and thence stowed by underslung internal cranes each capable of taking up to a ton of merchandise at a time and of conveying it and stacking it in any part of the shed. These cranes can hoist, slew, traverse, travel and derrick and can take from or deliver to road or rail from either side of the building they serve. The South Quay of the dock is laid out in a novel manner, seven dolphins being placed at a distance of thirty-two feet from the quay opposite to each shed. Vessels are berthed at the outside of the dolphins, on which are placed forty-nine cranes, while barges are berthed between the dolphins and the quays. This arrangement enables discharging and loading operations to proceed simultaneously to barges on each side of the ship or to the quay where two lines of rails facilitate the handling of railway traffic.

Besides the seventy-six electric cranes capable of handling three to five tons in the King George V Dock there are also forty in the Royal Victoria Dock and another ninety-five in the Royal Albert Dock, all of the same capacity, giving a total for the group of 211. The sight of them at work is one of the wonders of the modern industrial world. Here is 'the principal centre of London's commerce and the brightest jewel in the crown of Father Thames'.

*   *   *

Even nearer the centre of London—distant a matter of three miles—are situated the docks of the India and Millwall group, contained in the great loop of the Thames between Poplar and Greenwich. The group comprises the West India Docks (Export and Import Docks), opened in 1802, the East India Docks opened in 1806, the Millwall Docks opened in 1868 and the South West India Dock formed by the widening of the City Canal in 1870. The old East India Export Dock has become the site of a new electricity power station and East India Import Dock is now devoted to the short-sea and coastal traffic, but the other four main docks situated in the Isle of Dogs accommodate deep-sea vessels, and have been made inter-connecting by a majestic scheme completed in 1929.

In the West India Docks the nine Georgian warehouses built by the architects Gwilt, father and son, along the North Quay of West India Import Dock had the largest continuous frontage of any buildings in Europe and even though war-time bombing has reduced this frontage from 2,800 to 600 feet the two surviving warehouses (now scheduled as buildings of architectural and historic interest) present a façade as big as that of Wentworth Woodhouse, the largest country house in Britain. The North Quay has always been dominated by that major West Indian product—sugar. In the old days one walked in the sheds upon a thick layer of sticky and aromatic sugar-droppings rolled hard by trucks and here, at the time of the blitz, the loss of the old Georgian sugar warehouses rivalled the destruction of the timber sheds at Surrey Commercial Docks as the biggest fire ever to have occurred in the docks. It is still a case of sugar and general cargo at the North Quay. The Rum Quay on the south side received two severe blows, the disastrous fire in 1933 (when rum to the value of £300,000 was destroyed) and the war-time bombing, which was mortal. The rum is now lightered to London Dock and stored in the Brandy Vaults. London's hardwood trade is centred at the Wood Wharves where large tonnages of heavy mahogany, greenheart and other hard-wood logs are manœuvred with ease in the great timber sheds by powerful gantry cranes.

On the south side of the Import Dock a splendid new quay has been laid down equipped with two huge, airy, three-storeyed brick and concrete warehouses 432 feet long and 128 feet wide. The doorways are 20 feet high to allow access for the mobile cranes and fork-lift trucks that con-stantly enter and re-enter them. Green and dried fruit and general cargo are efficiently handled here with mechanical aids.

At the west end of the South Quay fresh fruit from the Canary Islands is discharged at Canary Wharf into a modern warehouse complete with loading platforms, balconies and electric wall and quay cranes. Together with planned road and rail access the South Quay presents an excellent example of modern layout.

At 'H' Shed, South West India Dock, is the fully mechanized export berth where the trials were carried out which induced the Authority to proceed with its schemes for mechanization in other parts of the Port of London.

The West India Docks today still handle the general trade of the West Indies and Caribbean, as well as much trade from North and South America, East, West and South Africa, the Mediterranean, France, Spain, Portugal, China, Japan, Malaya and Hong Kong. Millwall Docks handle the Persian Gulf export traffic and the Scandinavian import and export traffic. The largest single commodity handled is bulk grain which is cascaded in rivers of gold from the ships' holds into barges or discharged into transit silos on the quayside or to the Central Granary by suction-machines, each capable of discharging at the rate of fifty or sixty tons an hour. The Central Granary can hold 24,000 tons of grain which is estimated to be about sufficient for London's needs for one week. The Granary and McDougall's flour-mill close by dominate the skyline of Millwall Docks.

*　　　　*　　　　*

One only of the Port of London's five dock systems lies to the south of the Thames—the Surrey Commercial in the great northward loop of the river between Limehouse Reach and the Lower Pool. Little more than a mile below Tower Bridge, spreading over 380 acres of Rotherhithe and comprising eleven docks with a total water-area of 136 acres, it is the centre of the softwood timber trade. The largest dock in the Surrey system, the Greenland Dock, was constructed in 1697 and remained practically unaltered until 1900, when it was enlarged and modernized in the last big development scheme carried out by private enterprise in the Port of London. Near it is the deepwater Quebec Dock with its six timber-discharging berths built by the P.L.A. between the wars. During the blitzes of the last war more than two hundred of the Surrey Commercial's timber sheds were destroyed or severely damaged. In replacing them, revolutionary designs have been adopted and the new sheds, while open at the ends like their predecessors to allow free circulation of air, are higher, with concreted floors and wide alleyways to accommodate the mobile cranes—more than fifty of them now at work—that have taken the place of the muscular and acrobatic deal porters who used to carry the timber from the quays and pile it, at risk to life and limb,

inside the sheds. These labour-saving machines are operated
by the latter's successors—dockers highly skilled in the
mechanical techniques demanded by their fast-evolving
profession. Some of the sheds are of tubular steel construction with specially enclosed sections designed for the handling
of plywood by fork-lift trucks. One of the largest is a two-
storey transit shed, 350 ft. long and 150 ft. wide, with water-
access on both sides, electric hoists for delivering cargo
from the upper storey and mechanical facilities for piling
general cargo on the ground floor to a height of 20 ft.
Altogether there is accommodation in the Surrey Commercial
Docks for over 83,000 standards of softwood and 22,000
tons of hardwood, as well as for more general merchandise
which is being shipped to this great south bank dock group
in increasing quantities. But its chief trade, as in the past,
continues to be with the Scandinavian and Baltic countries
and with Canada, Greenland and Russia.

*   *   *

The last to be reached of the P.L.A.'s dock groups are the
London and the St. Katharine Docks in the heart of the
metropolis and only just outside the liberties of the old
walled City of London. The main entrance to the London
Docks is at the eastern end of the Lower Pool, at Shadwell,
while the principal entrance to the St. Katharine Dock is
hard by the Tower Bridge. St. Katharine Dock adjoins but
is not connected to the London Dock. The two docks,
however, came under united control by amalgamation in
1864. The London Dock has been equipped in the last
decade with new approaches, cargo berths and transit sheds
of the most advanced kind. The London and St. Katharine
Docks system constitutes the smallest and most picturesque,
but by no means least important of the five dock groups.
In the value and variety of their wares and in the technical

intricacy of the services performed in their warehouses they
are second to none. Here is the home of the tea trade—where
in a specially reconstructed warehouse the Authority's staff
weigh, tare, sample, bulk and set out for inspection fine
oriental teas. London Dock is also the seat of the wool trade,
of the iodine trade, of London's and much of England's
import of wine and spirits. Here, too, are centred the storage
of veneers, plywood, canned goods, gums and wax and the
luxury traffic in perfumes and essential spirits, the seasonal
dried-fruit trades, the rubber trade and the ivory trade where
elephant tusks and rhinoceros horns are graded and displayed
before auction sales. Many of these commodities, brought
by larger vessels than the London Dock will accommodate,
are lightered upstream from the deeper docks lower down the
river. Here, too, many of them receive the skilled treatment
in handling and storing which they require and for which
the London Dock is specially equipped and staffed. Most of
them involve storage in premises where they cannot be
contaminated or spoilt, and all, because of their value, need
protection from theft and fire. Though no part of London
was more heavily bombed during the war, the vast fortress-
like warehouses erected to the east of the Tower by the rich
individualists of the early nineteenth century still afford
storage and maximum security to what has been described as
'the world's greatest concentration of portable wealth'.

In this 'massive safe deposit' more than a third of the
wool annually imported into the river is stored. On the
show floors of the Crescent Warehouse there is room for
17,000 bales, and buyers come from every part of Europe to
inspect the bales—cut open and displayed for them under
natural lighting—before attending the auctions of the
London Wool Exchange. The P.L.A.'s staff, acting both for
importers and purchasers, weigh, sample, lot, display, re-
class, re-bale and despatch the wool.

Equally remarkable is the work performed by the
Authority's craftsmen in gauging, recording, sampling,
blending, vatting, bottling, corking, capsuling, labelling and
casing the vast quantities of wine and spirits which arrive in
the Thames throughout the year from every wine-producing
country in the world. In one warehouse the Authority's
staff bottle for the Noilly Prat Company of France all the
vermouth they import into England; in two others—Nos. 4–5
Pennington Street—40,000 gallons of wine are normally
kept in stock. Under these London Dock warehouses are
vast vaults, more than twenty acres in extent, where a
constant temperature of 55° F. is maintained and where
brandy in cask acquires naturally over the years that
distinctive condition which only storage in such an ideally
controlled temperature can give. One firm of brandy
importers alone keeps an average of 40,000 cases of brandy
in bottles permanently in bond here, but recently had a peak
figure of 90,000 in storage, the duty payable on which
would amount to well over a million pounds. Rum lightered
from the West India Docks is stored in the Brandy Vaults and
also in the Virginia Street, and the East and West Vaults; the
present stock amounts to 53,000 barrels, valued, with customs
duty, at about 30 million pounds.

*   *   *

One last priceless treasure-house belonging to the P.L.A.
remains to be explored. The warehouses of the former East
India Company in Cutler Street have no visible connection
with the river from which their wealth flows; they lie in the
City itself, opposite Liverpool Street Station, largely hidden
by offices and shops, behind eighteenth-century walls. Here,
laid out on the fifteen acres of floor space of these huge
fortress-like warehouses, is wealth beyond the dreams of
avarice. Fine tea, which used to be housed here, was

transferred a few years ago to the London Dock, excepting for the Sample Distribution Centre, which is still in Cutler Street and where, under the control of the Tea Clearing Centre, samples from all London's twenty-four tea warehouses are received and sorted for the convenience of brokers and merchants. But its place has been taken by fine vintage wines, which are bottled and binned here by the Authority's cellarmen. Every year the contents of some two thousand pipes of vintage port and sherry are drawn off into bottles, corked, capsuled and labelled and either packed into cartons and despatched to their purchasers or binned in the P.L.A.'s bonded cellars, which are fitted with open steel racks and kept at an even temperature by thermostatic control. At the present time over three-quarters of a million bottles of vintage port and light wines are 'binned' here in the racks to allow the 'crust' of the vintage port to form and for the light wines to mature. A new Wine Bottling department has recently been opened for filtering and bottling French, German and Portuguese light wines, and much of the Burgundy drunk in England today is handled at Cutler Street Warehouses.

Another class of luxury goods housed in these unique warehouses is cigars. Between four and five million of these are normally kept in stock and are weighed and tared to the thousandth part of a pound by the Authority's craftsmen on behalf of importers before passing through the bond of the Customs authorities, whose rate of duty—£3 11s. 1d. per lb. —naturally necessitates the utmost degree of accuracy. Ostrich feathers and tortoise-shell, silks, rayon and nylons, mother-of-pearl, clocks, watches, cameras and musical instruments are among the valuables passing through Cutler Street and its vast bonded rooms. So are drugs, spices and perfumes, the names of which read almost like the catalogue of a magician's dispensary—cinchona bark for

making quinine; slippery elm, witch hazel and roots of
belladonna; squills, jalap, rhubarb root and ipecacuanha;
sarsaparilla, aloes, and dill; South American yerba maté for
tea-infusing, Russian foxglove for digitalis, passion flower
for sedatives; cloves, pepper, ginger, paprika and vanilloes;
musk pods from the musk-deer, ambergris from the bile of
the sperm whale, isinglass from the membrane of the great
sturgeon; myrrh, attar of roses and gum benjamin; gamboge
and dragon's blood for pigments and printer's ink; sun-
flower seeds for feeding parrots, cuttlefish for canaries, and
even dried water fleas—or daphnia—for goldfish!

It would be impossible to enumerate all the miscellaneous
articles—classified as 'General Goods'—which arrive by
sea and are housed in Cutler Street on account of their
special value, from works of art to sewing machines and
Chinese bristles for making paint brushes. One branch of
the work of Cutler Street consists of delivering to would-be
purchasers samples of a vast range of commodities that enter
the docks almost every day from every part of the world.
During 1957 alone nearly two hundred thousand samples
were sent out in its sample delivery vans to premises and
shops in the City and West End.

Perhaps the most romantic of all the goods that are housed
in and pass through Cutler Street are the Oriental carpets
and rugs which, since the end of the First World War, have
been sent from the East for safe storage and sale in London,
instead of, as formerly, to Constantinople. Thanks to the
P.L.A.'s foresight and enterprise and the exceptional security
and warehousing facilities it was able to offer when the
Turkish Empire collapsed in 1918, London became the
centre of a trade which historically and geographically
has always been associated with 'the gorgeous East' and
which is still conducted mostly by Armenian and other
Oriental dealers. They operate, not, as one would expect,

from Cairo, Calcutta or Smyrna, but from foggy Hounds-
ditch, and it is one of the many astonishing spectacles
afforded by a visit to the P.L.A.'s premises to see one of
these wise men of the East seated among his many-coloured
wares awaiting his clients or, as often as not, silently
contemplating the beauty and infinite variety of the stock he
has acquired by his knowledge and skill. Here buyers come
from every part of Europe, and even from Africa, South
America and the East itself, to buy the traditional crafts-
manship of Persia, Bokhara, Turkestan, India, Afghanistan
and China, stacked and spread out for inspection on the
floors of the 127 rooms—comprising eight acres of floor
space—devoted to this fascinating trade. Some of the rooms
are leased by individual merchants; anything from a hundred
thousand to a hundred and fifty thousand carpets and rugs
are normally stored here, the greater part being subsequently
re-exported. Some of the carpets, stacked upright in vast
rolls, measure forty or fifty feet long, while others—tiny
strips or saddlebags, often of exquisite workmanship and used
for upholstering chair backs and seats—are only a foot or
two square. All are documented by the warehouse staff and
distinguished by lettered and numbered labels bearing the
name of the ship in which they arrived in England. After
sale the P.L.A. staff pack them in bales for delivery or
re-export.

*   *   *

Such are the scope and work of the P.L.A.—though a brief
summary of this nature can indicate only a fraction of the vast
variety of goods the Port handles. Its business affects the life
of every Londoner and of every inhabitant of these islands.
Its national importance has been repeatedly acknow-
ledged, and symbolized by, the visits paid to it by
each one of the Sovereigns who have reigned during its

half-century of existence. On many occasions since the war
'the great street paved with water' which it administers has
been the scene of the traditional royal pomp and pageantry
so long associated with the Thames—notably at the time of
the Coronation and in the final episode of the Queen's
Commonwealth Tour in 1954, when, with Prince Philip,
Her Majesty disembarked from the Royal yacht, *Britannia*,
in the Pool of London after a triumphant progress up the
river from the Nore. On 12 May 1959, the Queen and Prince
Philip honoured the Port by their presence at the Authority's
Jubilee celebrations, and, after lunching with the Members
of the Board at the Head Office, had a wonderful reception
from thousands of dock workers while they inspected the
London Docks, the Royal Victoria, the Royal Albert and the
King George V Docks, afterwards embarking in the P.L.A.
yacht, *St. Katharine*, to see the congregation of great ships
in the Royal Docks and to return up the beflagged river from
Gallions Reach to Tower Pier and thence to proceed home,
in the motor-launch *Nore*, to Westminster.

   To understand the significance and the history of the Port
of London, one should stand on a winter's afternoon at the
foot of the great steps below the main entrance of the
Authority's Head Offices in Trinity Square and look around.
To the east is the low classical façade of Trinity House,
home of the seafarer's craft or mystery that has continued
for close on five hundred years of unbroken history and with
which the P.L.A.'s work on the river is intimately linked.
To the north, hidden by the great building behind, is Pepys
Street and the open space once occupied by the East India
Company's Warehouse and, earlier, by the Monastery of the
Crutched Friars; beyond is the street of Crutched Friars,
with Seething Lane to the west, where Pepys lived and
worshipped in the Church of St. Olave's, Hart Street. Here
also, a century before, the great Elizabethan statesman, Sir

Francis Walsingham, lived and the Admiral who commanded the English Fleet that defeated the Spanish Armada, Lord Howard of Effingham. To the south are the Conqueror's Tower flying the Union flag, the turrets of Tower Bridge, the dark river and, beyond, the cranes of the Surrey wharves gaunt against the sky. And in the immediate foreground, between them and the P.L.A. Building, is the green grass of Tower Hill where, in that small space, between 1388 and 1747 so many of the noblest heads in England fell on the scaffold, and where today stands the memorial to the British merchant seamen and fishermen who gave their lives in two world wars—twelve thousand in the first and twice that number in the second, all of whose names and those of their ships are here recorded, and who, as the plaque commemorates, 'have no grave but the sea'. Like the Tower of London beside it the memorial 'tells of duty done and duty doing'.

South of the Port of London Building is All Hallows Barking, the oldest church in the City, whose Vicar for thirty-eight years, the Reverend P. B. Clayton, is Hon. Chaplain to the Authority. Founded in 675 the church was saved from the Great Fire of London in 1666 by Samuel Pepys but was almost destroyed in the blitz of 1940, apart from its tower, ancient crypt and undercroft and has now been lovingly rebuilt with the addition of a fine spire, largely the gift of Sir Ion Hamilton Benn, a churchwarden who also has been a Member of the Port of London Authority for fifty-one years.

To all this and the agelong life of the river below, the Port of London Authority is heir—this twentieth-century giant which administers the trade and traffic of the greatest port in the world and yet which, on midsummer day, 'upon the Festival of St. John the Baptist', presents to the Lord Mayor of London a rose 'fresh pluckt' from its garden in Seething Lane as quit rent for a breach of the City building regulations committed six hundred years ago by its then predecessor in title of this land, Sir Robert Knollys, a valiant soldier and former citizen who fought in the wars of Edward III and the Black Prince.

INDEX